LONG SHOT

LONG SHOT

My Life As a Sniper in
the Fight Against ISIS

AZAD CUDI

WEIDENFELD & NICOLSON

First published in Great Britain in 2019 by Weidenfeld & Nicolson
an imprint of The Orion Publishing Group Ltd
Carmelite House, 50 Victoria Embankment
London EC4Y 0DZ

An Hachette UK Company

1 3 5 7 9 10 8 6 4 2

A CIP catalogue record for this book is
available from the British Library.

ISBN (Hardback) 978-1-4746-0977-7
ISBN (Export Trade Paperback) 978-1-4746-0978-4
ISBN (eBook) 978-1-4746-0980-7

Typeset by Input Data Services Ltd, Somerset

Printed and bound by CPI Group (UK) Ltd, Croydon, CR0 4YY

www.orionbooks.co.uk

For all freedom's martyrs who came before us,
and for the thousands who fell in Kobani

Contents

Author's Note

My account of the 2013–2016 war against ISIS and, in particular, the five months of resistance in Kobani from late 2014 to early 2015 is based on my personal experience. I made extensive notes during the year I spent in Kobani immediately after my part in the fighting was over. Since then, I have consulted my comrades for their recollections, made free use of what records were kept by the YPG and YPJ, sought out official records from the US Department of Defense, interviewed historians, activists and journalists, and cross-referenced everything with media reports from the time. Any errors that remain are my own.

I am aware, of course, that while the essential facts of when and where ISIS' advance across the Middle East was halted and reversed are well known, the story of how it happened on the ground is one hitherto untold. That is largely because so many of those who took part in those events did not survive them. It is my fallen comrades, above all, who have been my guide in these pages.

Leeds
February 2019

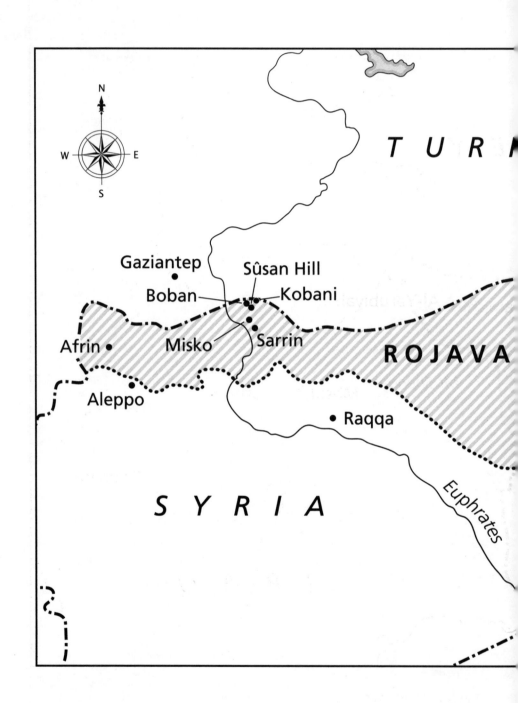

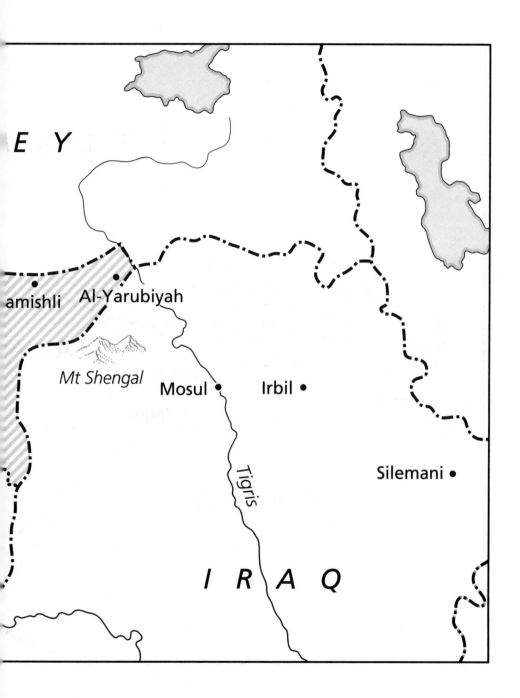

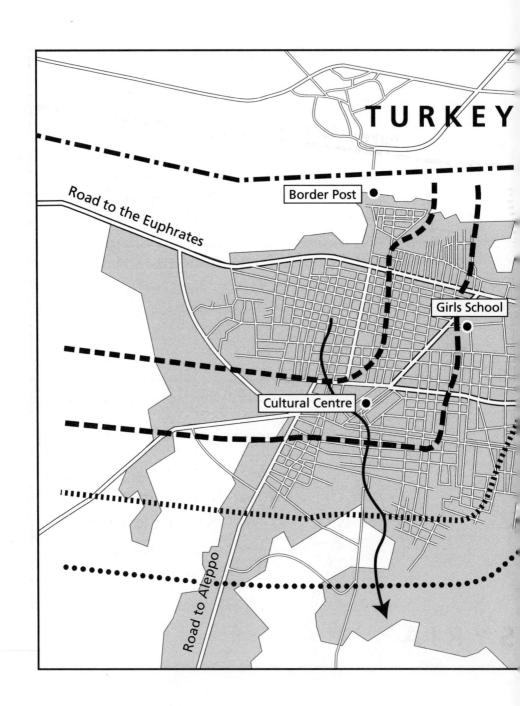

TURKEY

Border Post

Road to the Euphrates

Girls School

Cultural Centre

Road to Aleppo

Turkey – Syria border

Kobani

N
W — E
S

Black School

48th Street

SYRIA

←	Sneaking behind enemy lines, October 2014
▬ ▬ ▬	Initial line of honour, October 2014
▬ ▬ ▬	November 2014 front
▪▪▪▪▪▪▪▪	December 2014 front
●●●●●●	Mid January 2015 front

Liberation of Kobani, 27 January 2015

ONE

Outside Sarrin, southern Rojava,

April 2015

I have had many names – Sora as a boy in Kurdistan, Darren in my British passport – but as a sniper I went by Azad, which means 'free' or 'freedom' in Kurdish. During the war, my name would remind me of a Kurdish saying: that the tree of freedom is watered with blood. It's a proverb about righteous sacrifice, about how liberty is never easily given but requires long and painful struggle. And perhaps one day enough of our women and men will have fought and died that we will live in a world of peace, equality and dignity, drinking water from the mountain spring and eating mulberries from the trees. But Kobani was not that world. In Kobani, we lost thousands and we killed thousands – and it was like that, feeding the earth of our homeland, drop by drop, that we nursed and raised our freedom.

I had been fighting for sixteen months in Kurdish territory in northern Syria by the day in April 2015 when I was asked to leave my position on the eastern front, close to the Turkish border, and join an advance on our southwestern one. We had recaptured Kobani in January. In the battles since, we had pushed the jihadis back far enough in every direction that

1

crossing our territory was no longer a short dash through the streets but a five-hour drive across open country. As we set off, to the north across the Turkish border, I could make out the snowy peaks where they say Noah beached his ark. Below them, rolling towards us, were the wide, grassy valleys and pine forests of Mesopotamia, the land between the Euphrates and the Tigris where our people have lived for fifteen thousand years. As we drove further south, the slopes eased into prairie farms and bare-earth hills that rose and fell like the swell on a big sea. When the sun began to dip, I watched the late afternoon light play on the last of the apricot blossom and the red and yellow poppies by the side of the road.

Soon it was dark. The old farmer's pickup in which I was travelling was in a terrible condition – no suspension nor lights nor much tread on its tyres – and the roads were rutted and slippery. I am not sure we managed more than twenty miles an hour the entire journey. At one point, we came across a group of our women comrades sitting around a fire and stopped for a glass of black tea. Finally, at 11 p.m., long after I was numb with bruises, we arrived at a small settlement of fifty mud-walled houses, some of them bearing the familiar signs of invasion: bullet holes, RPG splashes and the jihadis' black graffiti. There I was asked to a briefing with the commanding officer, General Medya.

Medya was in her thirties and a veteran of more than a decade of fighting. She went into battle with her long black hair tied back in a ponytail and a green headscarf tugged down above her one working blue eye. One thing that outsiders always find surprising about the Kurdish resistance movement is our insistence that women and men are equal in all things, including war. In our People's Protection Units, a volunteer has to be eighteen to pick up a gun but otherwise all that matters to us is whether you are sharp and useful, not where you are from and certainly not the accident of your gender. Men and women fight alongside each other in separate entities: the YPJ, or Yekîneyên Parastina Jin (pronounced *yek-een-ayen para-steena jin*), for women; and the YPG, or Yekîneyên Parastina Gel (pronounced *yek-een-ayen para-steena ghel*), for men. And the women fight, kill and die as hard as the men, as ISIS can attest. We often talked about how confused the Islamists must have been to find a woman standing over them in their last moments. If they left this earth in doubt, then it made us doubly sure that we were the perfect army to defeat them.

Medya began by saying that the day of our liberation was at hand. The moment we took back the last yard of our homeland would be the one in which we saved our people. It would also be the day that civilisation and progress triumphed over the medieval backwardness of the jihadis. Though they would never admit it, we would be achieving what the great nations of Europe and the Americas could not. We would even be saving our oppressors in Turkey, Syria, Iraq and Iran. And with our victory, we would finally bring due attention and support to our cause of an autonomous Kurdistan.

For that great day to arrive, said Medya, these last advances had to succeed. Our next immediate objective was a fortified ISIS base on a hill outside the northern Syrian city of Sarrin. Taking it would be best done at night, and that would require a sniper with a thermal scope to lead the attack. 'The hill you are to capture is about two kilometres in this direction,' Medya told me, pointing to the south. 'To take it, you must first climb another one next to it from where you can fire across at them. There might be fifty of them. We think there are only a handful. Arrive, assess the situation and proceed.'

Medya led me over to meet the small team I would be

3

taking. Leaning up against a wall holding his Kalashnikov was Xabat, perhaps twenty-one, who spoke clearly and with great enthusiasm and who had scouted the hills we were to attack earlier that day. There was a second man with a Kalashnikov, dark and skinny, who said nothing. There was a short, strong woman with a round face called Havin, who carried an RPG launcher. She had a loader, a nineteen-year-old man who carried her spare rockets and radio. Completing the squad was an older guy, Shiro, maybe twenty-eight or twenty-nine, skinny, tall, unshaven, with thinning long hair, who carried the BKC, a 7.62-calibre machine gun.

It felt like a good team. When I walked towards them, they turned to me. When I regarded them, they looked back at me with clear and steady eyes. We introduced ourselves and shook hands. I checked my kit – one spare night-scope battery, two grenades in my vest, five M16 mags filled with thirty cartridges each – and we set off.

For a daytime assault, a sniper picks a high place like a building or a hill and covers the advancing soldiers from behind. At night, however, a sniper with night vision leads the attack because only he can see the target. That night, the moon was just a thin crescent. Everyone in the team would be blind except me.

To advance to the first hill, we followed an established procedure. I walked ahead two or three hundred metres, checked it was clear and, after finding cover, said 'Now!' into the radio, which was the signal for the others to join me. We repeated this manoeuvre seven or eight times and were around five hundred metres from the first hill when we came under fire. I could hear the sharp, hollow sound of gunshots in the distance, then *fzzz fzzz*, like the sound of a honeybee, as the bullets passed overhead. Though the incoming fire forced us to drop to a crawl, in other ways it was useful. We had been quiet on our approach, which meant ISIS had to have night vision to have been alerted to our advance. If their bullets were passing over our heads, however, that suggested that the jihadis didn't have night scopes on their weapons, only a pair of binoculars. The sound of the fire also indicated only a handful of men, ten at the most, which meant we were evenly matched.

At 1.30 a.m., still under fire, we reached the top of the first hill. I could see there was a cairn at the summit where the farmers had stacked the stones they cleared from their fields. I stopped about fifty or sixty metres before the rock pile and called Xabat to join me. 'It's probably booby-trapped,' he said as he crawled up to me. As Xabat spoke, there was another burst from the ISIS positions and more *fzzz* sounds over our heads. We were getting closer.

Leaving the team behind a boulder, I stood up quite openly and, in full view of the ISIS fighters, walked briskly towards the cairn. When I reached it, I stopped for a moment to make sure they had seen me. Then I dropped down as though I was taking cover and crawled back the way I had come. Back behind a rock, I waited. If ISIS had mined the cairn, they would wait for all six of us to assemble next to it before they detonated it. In the end, the jihadis waited seven full minutes.

An explosion up close initially feels like your inner ears are being peeled. A split second later, you suffer a mini blackout as the blast wave hits your brain. You must keep your mouth open to allow the pressure to travel through you. If the detonation is truly close, you will probably reboot to discover that you are rag-dolling through the air, your nose, eyes and mouth filled with dust. If you are further away, it will be the earth that you feel bouncing. Next comes a shower of pebbles. Through all of it, there is nothing to be done but close your eyes and trust your luck. If you are going to die, it will be quick, as you are caught by the blast or hit by debris or smashed up against a wall or a rock. If you find yourself conscious and hugging the ground, unless something heavy lands on you, you're going to live. I remember the earth flexing, rocks shooting past our heads and pebbles raining down on us. We jammed our eyes and mouths into our elbows.

As the air cleared, my radio shrieked. 'Are you OK? Are you OK?'

It was General Medya.

'Fine,' I replied. 'Remote-control mine. They didn't get us.'

Through the dust, I could see Xabat grinning. 'I told you it was a booby-trap,' he said.

'Now,' I said into the radio. The team came up behind me and, as one, all six of us moved forward to what was left of the cairn.

At our new position, I told the others to place a few stones in front of them for cover. I took three rocks, arranged them under my rifle and pulled my scarf tightly around my head to hide the light from the night scope. Once I was satisfied I was concealed, I turned it on.

I saw them immediately. Through the thermal, I could make out a rock-walled base on a slope near the top of the hill opposite us, about five hundred and fifty metres away. As I scanned the area, I could see a skinny figure standing a few metres below the base, his heat image shining like a moon in the night. Three more men – one tall, one medium in height and a stocky man dressed in a long flowing shirt – were grouped together a few feet away. The skinny man was talking. The other three were listening. All four were out in the open.

The skinny one is the commander, I thought. *He is giving instructions. He is in charge.*

Five hundred and fifty metres is close range for a sniper. There was no need to adjust for wind. With a bullet travelling at seven hundred and sixty-two metres per second, the round would hit Skinny three quarters of a second after it left my barrel. The trigger on an M16 is also very quick. You just tense and it fires. I went for Skinny's head.

The stock punched my shoulder. Through my scope, I saw Skinny's head jerk away from me and his legs fall open. Then, as though he were a burst balloon, he deflated, slumping limply against a rock, his head on his chest.

I turned to the three other jihadis. Tall was trying to take cover behind some stones to the right. Medium Size and Long Shirt were running back up the hill towards the base. Medium Size stopped for a second. I aimed for his chest and tensed. Another kick. Medium Size was down.

Long Shirt was still running away up the hill. I followed him in my sights. When he stopped to pick up a large machine gun, I aimed for his body. Punch. Punch. The sound of my shots echoed off the rocks as Long Shirt went down.

I looked for Tall. He was over to the right, jumping from one boulder to another. He fired back at me but his aim was wild – just spray and pray. Behind the rocks, I could see part of his head and chest and one of his legs. I went for the leg. Punch. Tall fell to the ground, then started dragging himself to cover.

Now I could see a fifth man, short and fat, inside the base. Every now and then Fat Man would peek out over the wall, his round head appearing for a second, then he would disappear. I shot at him twice but he kept vanishing. He would show himself, fire a burst, disappear, then reappear at another place and fire once more.

7

I moved back to Tall. He was crawling in the dirt. He might have been trying to flank us. I told Havin, our RPG gunner, to move forward so she had a clear line of fire down the hill should he try to come up at us. I waited several minutes until Tall's head appeared between two rocks, then fired. His head tore away from me, pulling his body into a somersault and flipping him on his back. Tall was finished.

To the left, I could see Long Shirt was moving again, trying to hide behind a boulder. I switched my M16 to rapid fire to scare him into the open. I fired a burst, then another, then a third. But when I went to shoot a fourth time, my weapon jammed.

I removed the magazine, took my cleaning rod from my pack, lowered it into the gun, pushed the bullet out, put the mag back in and pulled the mechanism back to a firing position. Once again, it failed to load.

I turned off the scope, sat back on my knees, took off my headscarf and smoothed the material on the ground in front of me. Then I closed my eyes and exhaled. Keeping my eyes closed as we had been trained, I picked up the gun, removed the magazine, detached the stock, trigger and pistol grip from the barrel, then separated the charging handle and finally the bolt carrier. I laid everything in order on the scarf. Then I reversed the order – bolt carrier, charging handle, pistol grip, trigger and stock – until I had put the gun back together again. As I was finishing, Fat Man seemed to see me. He began shooting, his rounds slapping the rocks around me, sending burning needles of stone into my left leg.

The disassembly and reassembly took me two minutes. I opened my eyes and pulled back the release. There was nothing wrong with this gun. I put the magazine back in, and through the noise of Fat Man's assault heard the faint twang of a loose wire coil. *That* was the problem. If the magazine's internal spring had come loose, it wouldn't be pushing cartridges into the breech. I released the faulty mag, put it to one side, picked up a fresh one, slid it in and pulled back the release. *Shtick.* The exquisite sound of a round being securely chambered.

My pause had given Fat Man and Long Shirt time to breathe. Their bullets were coming in regularly now. A rocket grenade roared over our heads and exploded just behind us, the blast rinsing us with dirt and shingle. Xabat stood up and returned fire. Shiro started firing the BKC. I shrouded myself with my scarf once more and turned my scope back on.

Long Shirt had moved twenty to thirty metres down the hill. I fired the moment I saw him. He went down clutching his head and crying out '*Allahu Akbar! Allahu Akbar!*' This was their battle cry. But Long Shirt's voice was weak and I guessed he was bleeding out. Havin ululated back at him. 'Wuh-wuh-wuh-wuh-wuh!' she sang, using her hand. 'Wuh-wuh-wuh-wuh-wuh! *Biji reber Apo!* [Long live leader Apo!]'

To the left, I saw some movement from Skinny. He was on his back. One leg was lying flat on the ground but the other was moving up and down. I fired at the still leg. The other one kept moving, then dropped abruptly to the ground. Skinny was finished.

We had been in combat for fifty minutes. Four enemy were down. Only Fat Man remained. I asked Havin to fire at the walls behind which he was sheltering. With her first rocket, she hit the corner. The next went over. The third just below. I told Shiro to advance fifty metres down the hill and open fire. Then Fat Man would return fire, and show himself, and I would have him.

Shiro did as I asked, Fat Man stood up and I fired – but again he was too quick, ducking back down before I could get off my shot. Fat Man was defending himself well. He fascinated me, in a way. His comrades were all dead. But he was not leaving his position.

Xabat suggested that he and Shiro crawl around behind the base and attack it with grenades. It took them twenty minutes to reach the bottom of the hill. I kept firing so that Fat Man stayed low and did not spot them. But he guessed anyway. When Xabat and Shiro were a hundred metres in front of him, he detonated another mine. From my position, the explosion appeared to go off underneath them. But when the smoke cleared, I could see them crawling uphill, still unharmed.

'How's it progressing?' came Medya's voice on the radio.

'Nearly there,' I said.

When our men began circling around behind him, Fat Man heard them. It sent him into a panic. He kept sprinting outside, trying to spot them in the dark, then running back. I was following him and harassing him with short bursts, trying to make it impossible for him to shoot. When Xabat and Shiro were less than thirty metres behind the base, they called me.

'Fire more, please.'

As I shot several bursts, Xabat and Shiro ran towards the base and threw two grenades inside. There were two explosions. We waited for a minute. Silence.

I picked up my rifle, walked down the hill and up to the ISIS positions. Skinny, whom I had taken to be the commander, turned out to be the youngest. I had shot him in the head and the leg. Tall, Medium Size and Long Shirt were all in their late thirties. I had hit Tall three times in the leg and once in the head. Medium Size had bullet wounds in his shoulder, kidney, stomach and knee. I had hit Long Shirt in the head and neck. What remained of Fat Man after two grenades suggested he was the oldest, perhaps fifty, and probably in charge. He had died a captain's death, going down with his men.

Medya released me from duty and I walked alone back over the hills, through the boulders and thorn scrub that filled the valleys, until I arrived back at the village where I had left the pick-up. I packed up my gear and we drove the five hours back to the eastern front. The sky was brightening and through the morning fog I could see Sarrin in the distance. In the still of the dawn, with the battle ebbing in my veins, there was a tranquillity to the way these southern flatlands rolled gently down to the Euphrates. The houses were modest and purposeful: plain stone walls, a roof, windows and small wire chicken pens to the side. As the car descended into the valleys, kicking up pale dust as soft as flour, I have a memory of small clutches of pink and blue daisies appearing on either side of us.

In our movement, we trust each other to do the right thing. I knew it was my duty to fight on. I also knew my experience was needed. Over the last year, fighting had become so easy for me. All that time, I had kept just two questions in my mind. How are we going to attack them? And: how are they going to attack us? I squeezed all my past, present and future into answering them. Night after night, day after day, month after month, I had lain behind my rifle. Through scorching summers, chilling autumns, endless winters and wet, numbing springs, I had kept the enemy in my crosshairs. I had burned my eyes with looking. I had survived other snipers, gun attacks, suicide bombers, tanks, mortars, rocket grenades, booby-traps, trip-wires, stray air strikes, artillery strikes, heavy machine guns and remote-control mines. On a diet of scavenged cheese, jam, the occasional yoghurt and biscuits, I had wasted away to the weight of a thirteen-year-old boy. Without sleep, I lurked in the abyss between adrenalin and exhaustion. So many of my friends had died that I had acquired a new, unwanted duty: to survive in order to keep their memories alive. Observing, waiting, shooting – I packed all of life into that tight existence. If you had seen me back then, carrying my trigger finger through the sharp edges of war as though it were a baby, you would have understood that human beings can survive almost anything if they have purpose.

But lately I had begun to think that I had nothing left. I felt as though I had used up thirty or forty years of life in months. I was losing the ability to feel the passing of days. One misjudgement, one push too far, and the lone candle that remained in my soul would blow out and the darkness would eat me. Climbing up to the ISIS base outside Sarrin, I had felt myself falling asleep on my feet. The mud had sucked at me, drawing me into the earth's infinite embrace. Twice my team had called over to me as I drifted off to the side. At one point, Xabat had challenged me with his gun raised, suspicious of this wandering figure way off among the stones.

I had been back in my old position on the eastern front for a few days when General Tolin came to visit. 'It's good that you are here,' she told me. 'We need you here. How are you doing?'

'Coping,' I said.

Tolin nodded and sucked at her teeth. She looked off to the horizon. After a while, she said, 'Coping's not enough, Azad.'

I tried to reassure her. 'I can stay here,' I said. 'Here is OK for me.'

Tolin regarded me for a moment. She had made up her mind.

'You go back to Kobani,' she said. 'I will see you there.'

And like that my war was over.

TWO

Kobani,

December 2013 to April 2015

When the Islamic State of Iraq and Syria (ISIS) advanced into Kurdistan in December 2013, they might have expected to overrun us in days. Formed seven years earlier by a handful of inmates inside the crucibles of torture and humiliation that were the American prisoner-of-war camps in Iraq, ISIS was an evolution from al-Qaeda, established as an alternative for those who found Osama bin Laden's original group too tame.

The world hardly welcomed this new model of jihadi. But its retreat before ISIS suggested it largely accepted the Islamists' central contention: that no force on earth could match their vengeful, suicidal pathology. By the time ISIS invaded northern Syria, they were an army of tens of thousands on an unstoppable march across Iraq, Libya and Yemen, advancing in Afghanistan and Pakistan, and mushrooming in the Philippines, Algeria, Mali, Nigeria and Somalia. Even in places where the group had minimal presence, governments were spending billions trying to prevent attacks by its disciples, all the while resigning themselves to picking up the bodies after their failure.

For ISIS was no billionaire's plaything, no bomb-and-hide

operation run from a walled villa by a man who couldn't find the safety on a Kalashnikov. It was a sophisticated, proficient and well-resourced army. It borrowed skills, personnel and materiel from Saddam Hussein's old regime. It bankrolled itself to the tune of several billion dollars through taxes, donations, confiscations of businesses and the sale of pillaged oil and artefacts. It used its wealth to build a military stronger than many national armies, equipped with artillery, mortars, tanks and heavy machine guns, mobile battle kitchens and surgeries, even social media managers and investment specialists. And rather than al-Qaeda's few hundred members, ISIS was reinforced by thousands of foreign volunteers who flocked to it from Marseilles to Melbourne.

Of all the obstacles that stood in the jihadis' way, the tiny enclave that we had built around Kobani from the wreckage of the Syrian civil war was perhaps the least significant. Kobani was a small town of forty thousand people that you could cross on foot in thirty minutes. The area around it, which we called Rojava, was a thin, five-hundred-kilometre-long strip of bare-walled towns and mudbrick goat and wheat farms sitting below the border with Turkey. When civil war engulfed Syria in 2011, it was here that the Kurds had first risen up. In July 2012, after the forces of Bashar al-Assad withdrew, it was here that they declared the creation of Rojava, an autonomous and democratic province of Syria. Yet while we had our own frontiers and civil administrators, our defences were all but non-existent. We possessed just a few thousand young men and women volunteers. We had almost no money and lacked the most basic equipment, right down to binoculars and radios. What guns we had were generally older than we were.

But in Kobani, between September 2014 and January 2015, around two thousand of our men and women stopped ISIS' twelve thousand. Six months later, we pushed all the jihadis out of Rojava. Our defeat of ISIS set in motion their collapse. By early 2017, the jihadis' dream of a new caliphate had been squeezed to a few pinheads on a map and almost all of ISIS' foreign volunteers were either dead or fleeing the Middle East in their thousands.

How did we do it? When you hear that Nasrin shot two hundred jihadis, I shot two hundred and fifty, Hayri three hundred and fifty, and Yildiz and Herdem five hundred each – meaning the five of us took down a sixth of the army ISIS sent against us – you might think you have your answer. But, in truth, that was just one part of it.

The town where we made our stand, Kobani, wasn't much to look at. A collection of bare-brick houses clustered around a few dusty bazaars, it sat in a shallow valley surrounded by fields of dry, grey soil and pebbly semi-desert. In the late nineteenth century, Kobani had been a stop on the railway between Berlin and Baghdad. After the Allies redrew the map of the Middle East in 1916, the track was replaced with guard posts, fences and minefields – and what had once been a link between nations became an instrument of division. In the twentieth century, Kobani had eked out an existence as a small border town on the trade route between Arabia and Europe. Few of its people became rich, but no one starved, and most lived their whole lives there, learning in its schools, shopping in its markets and celebrating the spring festival, Newroz, in its squares.

Kobani's real significance was in its history. At its centre, archaeologists had found evidence of a dried-up oasis that once served herders moving their flocks between the Euphrates and the Tigris. Among them, supposedly, was Abraham, his wife Sarah and their son Isaac, who had lived for many years at Haran, a day's walk to the east, around 2,000 BCE. The archaeologists' digs showed that long before even that time, Kobani had been at the centre of the vast prairie of Mesopotamia. There, around thirteen thousand years ago, our ancestors had been among the first people on earth to give up wandering the land for food and, by domesticating sheep and goats and sowing wheat and barley, invent farming. Around Kobani, they established a homeland of grass-roof villages, and a mythology based around Nature and fertility. Historians called the area the Fertile Crescent. The Torah, the Bible and the Koran called it Eden.

In the year I spent in Kobani after General Tolin sent me back from the front, I came to realise that these terms were less descriptions of the land than a tribute to the people who had conjured forth a verdant paradise from the desert. The way Kobani sprang back to life after the war was astonishing. Each morning, the vegetable and fruit growers in the bazaars would construct displays so over-abundant as to suggest a lingering anxiety over whether this new-fangled idea called cultivation was going to work. Stalls would be piled high with lemons, prickly pears, pomegranates, black grapes and oranges, while small rockfalls of watermelons sat to the side. The next row would be a mosaic of turnips, potatoes, beetroots, carrots and white-and-fuchsia radishes. In another alley were the market's true giants: tomatoes the size of small pumpkins, and cucumbers, red and green peppers and shiny black aubergines the length of my forearm. These would be penned in by walls of lettuces, cabbages and cauliflowers and armfuls of coriander, spinach, mint, dill, rosemary and parsley. Yet another alley would be lined with buckets of green and black olives stuffed with chillies and garlic, great sacks of peanuts, walnuts, pistachios and

16

hazelnuts, and spice stalls heaped with miniature hills of dried chilli, scarlet paprika and golden turmeric.

As I wandered the markets, I inhaled the smell of sweet black tea, cigarette smoke, lamb stuffed with apricots and, my favourite, grouse roasted with honey and cinnamon. In the end, I came to see Kobani as a gigantic village. My alarm each morning was the sound of a cockerel. My view was a row of houses made of home-sawn wood and corrugated iron. Every backyard seemed to contain a cow or a goat.

When I think of how we withstood the Islamists, I think of Kobani's stubborn farmers. What anchored us all, fighters and farmers, was a connection to our land. With careful shepherding and untiring care, we had nurtured a rich and varied life from this meagre earth. The diversity was reflected in the city's population, a mongrel mix of Kurds, Armenians, Assyrians and Arabs, and a large population of Christians living alongside Sunni, Shia and Sufi Muslims, small communities of Sephardi and Musta'arabi Jews and even Zoroastrians.

Such a mosaic of humanity had often proved to be a recipe for division and conflict in the Middle East. Our intention, guided by the writings of our leader Abdullah Öcalan (also known as Apo), was to embrace it. By celebrating difference, and using tolerance to create community, we would break the cycle of tribe against tribe, and tyrant succeeding tyrant, and all the centuries of bloody murder and revenge that had scarred the region. Our plan was for an egalitarian, democratic society built on respect for all races, religions, communities, genders and nature. We rejected the patronising platitude, so common among Western commentators, that democracy and peace were alien to our land. We rejected, too, the notion that all freedom fighters were doomed to follow the same sorry path of liberating their people, only to turn around and oppress them.

17

And our ambition extended far beyond Rojava or Syria. The reason the Middle East was beset by continual war and crisis, we argued, was because it lacked an example of a peaceful, stable, free and fair society. Rojava was to be that beacon. Once we had planted the seed of liberty in every man and woman, our hope was that they would scatter it across the region and the world, just as they had sown the first grain in the first fields all those millennia ago.

To foreign observers used to labelling Middle Eastern movements with terms like 'religious', 'ethnic', 'socialist' or 'nationalist', we were, I think, a puzzle. Dogmatically broad-minded. Inflexibly anti-sectarian. Freedom fighters who eschewed power. Most confusingly, Middle Eastern *and* feminist. At the core of our philosophy was the conviction that all tribalism, injustice and inequality stemmed from an original act of oppression when man, the hunter-gatherer, abused his brute strength to violently subjugate his equal partner, woman. In a region where women had been enslaved by governments, culture and religion since time immemorial, in Rojava they were to be equal partners with men in marriage, faith, politics, law, business, the arts and the military. Some outside observers drew parallels to the Spanish revolution of the 1930s, which also united anarchists, communists, republicans and a vanguard of *mujeres libres* against fascism. We understood the comparison was intended as a compliment. But to us it underestimated what we were attempting: to end prejudice, free the downtrodden and allow the Middle East to escape the carnage that had gripped it for so long.

This was one reason why Kobani was about more than the achievements of a small band of snipers. Another reason was the courage and sacrifice of two thousand other men and women who fought there, many of whom I never met. All of them have their own tale of heroism. The stories of Herdem, Hayri, Yildiz, Nasrin and me are merely five in a library. To think of our use of sniping as some kind of brilliant tactic, or even a choice, would be misguided. If all you have is forty-year-old Kalashnikovs, a handful of hunting rifles and handmade grenades, your only option is to kill your enemy one by one.

But if you had seen me back then, lying out alone in the freezing ruins of Kobani, starved half to death, waiting days to take a single shot at a single man in an advancing army, I think you would have understood. This was about freedom and never giving up. The jihadis talked about commitment but their resolve was the swarm of the mob, a great wave smashing anything in its path. Ours was the grit of the barnacle, the wit and dexterity of David against Goliath. A good sniper understands craft and patience but great ones are masters of destinies, both their own and those of every person on the battlefield. Alone, you watch, decide and act. Alone, you end the other man. There are few purer expressions of free will in this world.

This unbreakable bond with liberty reflected the principles for which we fought and for which we were prepared to die. It also gave us a mental agility that was key to outwitting the automatons of ISIS. Rather than rely on some external code to guide our behaviour, we trusted in personal responsibility and self-discipline. Inside our military wings, there were no ranks, only operational leaders, and no orders, only suggestions. Nor did we see war as about heroes or glory or purifying fire, or even winning or losing, as ISIS did. War is the darkness in humankind's nature and the profanity in our imagination. It is a violation and an abomination. Only the malevolent or deranged would seek a war.

But with ISIS, malevolent and deranged were often what we faced. In many ways, the jihadis denoted the darkness in humanity. If we believed in human possibility, they took a more pessimistic view, regarding people as inherently corrupt and man-made progress as conceptually impossible. And since they reckoned that people couldn't be trusted to run their own affairs, ISIS had taken it upon themselves to keep them in line using the only language that sinners understood: repression. The jihadis imagined the otherworldly holiness of their cause excused them of any earthly morality. Democracy, equality, rights, tolerance, feminism, freedom – these were the pretty words Satan used to spread his corruption. The way to free people was, paradoxically, to make them servants to Allah and Islam. Likewise, if the first Muslims had been pure and the fourteen centuries since had been a corrosion, then the answer to humankind's arrogant, sinful advancement was a corrective, cleansing reverse.

These, then, were the stakes of our fight. Progress or regression. Light or dark. Life or death. Perhaps it was the way we held up a mirror to their craziness that persuaded the jihadis they had to crush us. For our part, though we would have settled for ISIS' withdrawal, we understood that there could be no accommodation with men who had given such free rein to their inner beasts.

And in Kobani, as perhaps nowhere else, we had a slim chance to stop them. ISIS had captured hundreds of towns, some of them with only a handful of men. That it had sent twelve thousand to attack this one town, and that we had deployed hundreds of men and women to defend it, reflected Kobani's strategic importance. If ISIS captured it, they would cut Rojava in two and take over a ninety-kilometre stretch of the Turkish border over which thousands more foreign jihadis could cross. They would also crush our dream of building a new democratic and free society in the Middle East.

But by committing so many men to Kobani, the jihadis unwittingly gave us an opportunity to defeat them. And as Vasily Zaytsev had shown in Stalingrad in 1942, when the enemy enters the city, a single unblinking sharp-shooter can keep an entire army in the dirt and change the course of a war. In Kobani there were five of us who could hit a man from a mile away. It was a moment that would never be repeated. In the months after Kobani, Hayri was killed, then Herdem, and as I write now it has been years since I have seen Yildiz and Nasrin. I alone am here to tell the story of how we stood our ground, took back our homeland street by street and house by house and, man by man, shot the jihadis to pieces.

THREE

Kobani,

September–October 2014

I first saw Kobani on an evening in September 2014. The sun was setting, the first hints of an autumn chill were stealing into the air and before me, about a mile away, ISIS was laying siege to the town with columns of fighters in pickup trucks, supported by heavy machine guns and tanks.

In the previous few days, ISIS had taken the three hundred and fifty villages that surrounded the town and advanced deep into its streets. Hundreds of our men and women were already dead. Some had made extraordinary sacrifices. One team commander called Cudi, facing a mass of advancing jihadis on a position called Sûsan Hill outside the city, had refused his general's suggestion to pull back. 'I can see the houses of Kobani from here,' he said over the radio. 'How can I leave? Their tanks will have to go over my body.' Minutes later, his commanders observed that, after wounding him, the jihadis did exactly as Cudi had predicted.

Arin Mikan, a platoon commander from the YPJ, the women's militia, made another extraordinary last stand. As ISIS advanced to her position on Mistenur Hill, the gateway to

Kobani, Arin told the women of her platoon to pull back. Then she strapped as many grenades and explosives as she could to her body, tied them to a single trigger and ran down the hill towards the jihadis. The Islamists tried to shoot her. Despite being hit several times, she kept running, crashed through their lines and pulled the detonator. Arin took ten jihadis with her when she died.

But ISIS had pressed on. Within days, they had pushed our surviving volunteers into a thin crescent of territory along the Turkish frontier that ran for several kilometres but was only about a dozen blocks from north to south at its widest point. Encircled as our forces were, the only way to join them was from Turkey. I followed the road to the border, eventually reaching an abandoned Syrian immigration checkpoint that consisted of a guardhouse and a pair of bruised and bullet-scarred gates, seemingly bent back by the maelstrom beyond. Squeezing between them and stepping out into the dusk, I found myself slipping and rolling on a carpet of bullet casings and unexploded mortars. I also came immediately under fire. I stumbled for cover and ran into the debris of collapsed walls, flattened houses and three-storey buildings that had vomited their insides into the street. Everywhere there was broken glass, splintered doors, burned earth, torched cars and soiled clothes. It was like a dark mirror of existence. The accessories of living were all around, yet life itself was absent. I stumbled on until I found my way to a basement in which a small group of our fighters were sheltering.

Kobani, I knew, was built on one of the oldest settlements on earth. It was astonishing how one week of war had erased so much history. Some of that was our doing. Talking to my comrades, I learned that since enemy snipers now had our entire territory within range, moving in the streets had become impossible. Instead our men and women were busy smashing through the walls of houses and shops and ancient bazaars to create a network of hidden, covered passageways. They were living and fighting in these tunnels, scurrying from a kitchen stacked with crockery and pots of rotting rice through a hole in a wall into a garden, then ducking back into the living room of a neighbouring house where a sofa might still sit in front of the television, a small bowl of dusty, shrivelled grapes to the side.

I became used to so much in the five months we fought in Kobani but I don't think I ever made peace with the way we robbed and vandalised these homes. We paved our passageways with prized carpets and precious mattresses so we could run without tripping over concrete and debris. Anything red we laid on top to conceal the blood that spilled from our wounded as they were dragged back from the front. I would desecrate children's brightly coloured bedrooms by smashing holes in their walls to make an aperture through which to fire. I would demolish kitchens, tables and wardrobes to find flat pieces of wood or marble on which I could lie behind my gun.

As I found my way through my new surroundings, I realised the war was suffocating all the colour in Kobani. Our green uniforms were covered in dirt. ISIS dressed in black. Everything else – the shops, the cars, the trees, the photographs of children on the walls, the tablecloths and bedspreads, the skirts and shirts on the washing lines – was being subsumed under a blanket of sticky yellow filth. With little to guide me through this monochrome wasteland, I found my way by smell as much as sight. The dull stink of unwashed bodies meant I was near the frontline. The sharp reek of bloating corpses told me that I was on it.

The only calm was what you could create in your mind. At night, I would lie out on the rooftops, listening to the flapping of the giant curtains that our volunteers stitched together out of sheets and prized rugs raided from closets and sitting rooms and hung across the streets to block ISIS' line of sight. The sound was like patchwork sails in a storm, and as I lay there, I would imagine I was a sailor out on deck, adrift on an ocean far away.

We all knew Kobani would be bloody. The jihadis had set the tone of the war from its first days in January 2014. They advanced by blitzkrieg, arriving in an overwhelming horde, subjecting us to an onslaught of artillery, tanks and mortars, then moving into the ruins to mop up survivors. In one early battle in eastern Rojava, in a place called Tel Hamees, ISIS pretended they were retreating to lure two hundred and fifty of our men and women into an open field that they had surrounded, then opened fire, tossed in hand grenades and finally waded through the bodies with swords, decapitating at will. Days later, when my comrades pushed ISIS out again, they found their friends' heads stacked up in piles like pomegranates on a street stall.

By the summer we had learned that such battlefield massacres were often just the start of ISIS' atrocities. Even against the dark record of fellow Islamists around the world, the jihadis distinguished themselves with their depravity and childlike simplicity. Here were grown men who roasted prisoners over fires and sold sex slaves with notes of provenance tied around their necks while carrying spoons into battle because of a fairytale they had been told about the feasts with the Prophet that awaited them in paradise. Their fighters made videos showing themselves executing hundreds of prisoners at a time by herding them into pits and opening fire. They filmed themselves beheading journalists, crucifying prisoners and throwing homosexuals from rooftops. They executed moderate imams and Christians for 'sorcery'. They sawed the heads off grandfathers just for daring to stay put in their homes when they invaded. They left hundreds of corpses piled high in central squares or hanging from lamp-posts. They paraded whole families through the streets, then gathered crowds to watch as they shot fathers in front of sons, sons in front of mothers, mothers in front of daughters and daughters in front of the bloody heap that had once been their families – and all this they broadcast on giant outdoor screens. They liked to say they would behead their enemies so swiftly that the first they would know of it was when their heads were on the ground and their eyes were looking back at their own feet.

That summer of 2014, the jihadis had attempted to escalate their butchery into a genocide. The Yazidis were Kurds, though with their own distinct origin, religion and culture, whose ancestral land in Iraq was just across the border from where I was initially stationed in eastern Rojava. From my sniper's nest in the town of Al-Yarubiyah, I could see across the frontier to the great edifice of Mount Shengal (Sinjiar in Arabic), to where the Yazidis had always retreated in times of trouble and where jihadis had surrounded tens or even hundreds of thousands of them with the intent of exterminating them.

Yazidis fleeing into our territory told us that ISIS had signalled the start of the massacre by issuing proclamations declaring them to be godless half-humans, a pollution on God's earth and undeserving of life. That was a cue for the jihadis to wipe out whole families and entire villages in an onslaught of blood and fire. If they took prisoners, it was only to extend their suffering. They demanded the men convert. If their captives refused, or sometimes even if they obeyed, they beheaded them

27

or lined them up and shot them en masse. In one massacre, the jihadis led a group of elderly men into an ancient Yazidi temple, only to blow it up with the old men inside. Just having hair under their arms was enough to condemn Yazidi boys to the same fate. The jihadis seemed to take particular pride in the ingenuity of their cruelty. Some men they led in chains to roundabouts, tied them to a stake and left them in the heat so they died of thirst in view of passing traffic. Others they herded into steel cages where they were burned alive or left to starve, or lowered into rivers to drown.

Some of the women were spared. A few were put to work as cleaners. But mainly these men of God took the women and girls as objects to be raped and passed around fighters. Gang-rape was routine. After the fighters were done, they would execute the women for licentiousness or sell them in the market as sex slaves. A few virgins were reserved for ISIS' business managers, who would sell them to rich Arabs for up to ten thousand dollars each.

Lest anyone imagine they were barbarians, ISIS had regulations for their trade in sex slaves. Some Yazidis brought us copies of an ISIS pamphlet entitled 'Questions and Answers On Taking Captives and Slaves'. It was permissible to have sex with a pre-pubescent girl, ISIS' leaders decreed, 'if she is fit for intercourse'. It was also legal to 'buy, sell or give' Yazidi females since, as unbelievers and sub-humans, 'they are merely property, which can be disposed of'. This also seemed to apply to the children that inevitably resulted from the jihadis' industrial-scale raping. These were taken away from their mothers as infants to be trained as Kurdish-looking suicide bombers who could infiltrate their own people.

One problem the jihadis encountered was that there were simply too many Yazidi women and girls for them to be able to rape or sell them all. The jihadis solved this conundrum by liquidating the excess. In the late summer of 2014 we heard about one massacre when ISIS, with an apparent eye on conserving labour and ammunition, buried alive hundreds of mothers with their children.

If there was a strategy behind this savagery, it was to persuade their enemies to flee. We did not. When ISIS advanced on Shengal, twelve of our volunteers set up on its summit and kept thousands of ISIS fighters at bay for days before they succumbed, allowing many hundreds of Yazidi families to escape. In the end, a total of five hundred thousand Yazidis fled to our territory or to Turkey. Still, the death and destruction were grotesque. ISIS killed around five thousand Yazidi men and abducted seven thousand women and children, most of whom remain missing to this day. Hundreds of Yazidi children died of thirst and starvation as they fled.

The Yazidis told us that scores of their women and girls had leapt to their death from the cliffs of Mount Shengal rather than let themselves be captured. As the jihadis switched the full force of their fury to us across the border in Syria, we soon had similar stories of our own. Arriving one afternoon in August 2014 in the town of Jazaa, not far from the Iraqi border, I found everyone talking about how three weeks before, when Jazaa had fallen to ISIS for the second time before being recaptured once again, a group of twelve young YPJ women defending a position on the rooftop of a two-storey building had fought to the end rather than let themselves be taken prisoner. When it became clear they were surrounded, they had gathered in a circle and pulled the pins on the grenades that each had kept for the purpose.

The story stunned me. Like many comrades, I carried three bullets in my breast pocket, one for each calibre of rifle, so that I would always be able to take my own life rather than be taken prisoner. We called these rounds our 'saviour bullets'. They gave us a sense of indomitable will. We alone would decide how we lived and how we died. I had already come across the bodies of comrades who had used their saviour bullets. One man was sitting down, his finger still on the trigger. One woman had tied her hand to her rifle. But saviour bullets were neat and precise and left a body for comrades to bury and a grave for relatives to visit. Grenades disintegrated you. It would be like you never existed.

I walked into the ground floor of the building where the women had died to find piles of clothes – soft fabrics in cheerful pinks, purples and greens – drenched in blood on the floor. There was a guard on duty. He told me the women had died on the second-floor roof terrace. I would have to go up there alone. 'I can't look at that again,' he said.

I climbed the stairs. The entire terrace was covered in a thick film of blood, some dry, some still wet, like the floor of an abattoir. All around were pieces of flesh and clumps of hair. There was a black ponytail, its tie still around it. On the walls was more hair, and on the parapet a few scattered wisps trembling in the wind. These young women would have known their fate if they were captured by ISIS. The story went that they decided they couldn't allow the jihadis to use their bodies in any way, not even allowing them the fleeting pleasure of a glimpse of their beauty.

I was still on the roof, trying to digest the power of what I was seeing, when General Qahraman, commander of our eastern front, climbed up and gingerly moved to a corner to get a signal on his phone. All week Qahraman had been calling

Kobani. That day, as Qahraman listened to the voice on his phone, his shoulders slumped. When he hung up, he said the latest information was that our forces were down to their last few hundred yards and ISIS was hours from capturing Kobani.

I looked around the rooftop. It wasn't that anyone wanted to die. But war had been thrust upon us and suicidal defiance often seemed the only response we had. We all knew we would face injury, horror and death – and we set our minds to sharing these things with our comrades. Using a Kurdish saying, we said we embraced the moment with 'wild flowers and mint'.

I also knew I would be useful in Kobani. In eight months, I had shot around fifty ISIS fighters: fifteen kills I had confirmed with my own eyes and around thirty-five probables. I hated the body counts. Only a weak man would measure himself in kills and only a fool would try to describe all the hate, loss, sacrifice and love in war with a number. But like the women of Jazaa, I knew there were times when extreme actions were necessary. I told Qahraman I would go to Kobani to assist the resistance.

He nodded. 'Try not to get killed in the first three days,' he said.

As I made my home in the ruins of Kobani, I was happy to come across a familiar face. But whereas General Tolin had been warm and positive when I first met her months earlier in eastern Rojava, now, at a briefing for new arrivals, her face was tight and focused. She went around our small group, asking each man and woman their names and skills. Then she summarised the situation. There were three fronts – east, south and west. All of them were backed up against the Turkish border to the north and barely three hundred metres at their widest. 'We have run out of space to retreat,' she said. 'Our frontline is now a line of honour. We hold it or we die fighting. This will be our legacy to our fellow Kurds.'

Tolin said each front was defended by around one hundred and fifty men and women, broken down into three platoons of fifty, each of those made up of four or five squads or teams. Ideally, each team would have a heavy machine gun, an RPG, a medic and a sniper as well as four or five fighters with Kalashnikovs. But after so many casualties, most were several bodies short, with barely enough guns to go around. Tolin assigned the new volunteers to fill the gaps as best she could. When she came to me, she asked me to stay behind.

After the others had left, Tolin said she was dispatching a special operation of seventy men and women to cross secretly over our front and into enemy territory. There, in the villages and fields deep behind their lines, we were to run sabotage operations to create confusion and paranoia among the jihadis by showing we could live fearlessly among them, killing them at will. Though Tolin didn't say it, we both knew it was potentially a suicide mission. If ISIS found or captured us – if any of us made one small noise or movement at the wrong moment – it would be over for all of us.

The mission required two snipers to back up the main force, which would be divided into small teams of three to seven people. I suggested I go with another experienced marksman from Jazaa. When I went to retrieve a rifle for each of us, however, all I could find were two badly damaged Kalashnikovs. I was about to query Tolin when she interrupted me. 'Ah, Azad,' she said. 'I see you found your weapon.'

I looked at the battered gun in my hands. 'I can't use this,' I said. 'I couldn't even kill myself with this.'

Tolin pulled a ball-shaped object from her waistband and gave it to me. In my hand I held a mass of nails taped to a stick of dynamite, with a string fuse hanging to the side. Tolin took my free hand and slapped a plastic lighter into it. 'Welcome to Kobani, comrade,' she said.

FOUR

Britain and Sweden, *2004–2013*
Rojava, *September–December 2013*

It was almost exactly a year since I had arrived in Rojava as a volunteer civil administrator. To return to the Middle East a decade after fleeing as a twenty-year-old Iranian army deserter and political dissident might make little sense to some. After all, my family had borrowed everything they could to smuggle me to Europe. In Britain, I had found asylum. In Leeds, and later Stockholm, I had found a new home and a new, free life. But in my time away I had become convinced that I couldn't live in comfort while my brothers and sisters tried to build a new homeland. In particular, I had been deeply affected by the writings of the leader of the Kurdish Workers Party, or PKK, Abdullah Öcalan.

Apo, as we called him, using the ward for 'uncle' in Kurdish, had first emerged as a leftist student leader in Turkey in the 1970s. Initially, he proposed that the Kurds should violently overthrow centuries of repression by the Turks before going on to reunite their homeland, which lay divided between Turkey, Iran, Iraq and Syria. He had remained a radical until his early fifties, leading the Kurdish struggle from exile. But in February

1999, he was in Kenya en route to South Africa at the invitation of Nelson Mandela when he was kidnapped with the assistance of the American, Israeli and Turkish intelligence agencies and handed back to Turkey.

Kurds erupted in outraged protest around the world. American, Israeli, Turkish and European embassies and political party offices were picketed and occupied. Around ninety demonstrators set themselves on fire, several dying of their injuries. In Turkey, Kurds rioted across the country, battling police and petrol-bombing vehicles, and more than a thousand were arrested.

The Turks, like the apartheid authorities in South Africa, viewed revolution as a virus. Just as the white supremacists tried to hinder its transmission by quarantining Mandela and other African National Congress leaders on Robben Island off Cape Town, so the Turks transported Apo to the tiny island of Imrali off Istanbul where they built him a prison in which he was the sole inmate, guarded by hundreds of soldiers who were forbidden to talk to him.

But the Turks underestimated Apo. After his lawyers won him the right to read and write to prepare his appeal against his imprisonment, Apo built himself a prison library in which he dedicated himself to study and thought, and the preparation of a grand defence that took in thousands of years of history and philosophy. He was said to have read more than three thousand books. He set out the case for his defence in eleven books and pamphlets of his own.

What emerged, by the spring of 2004, the year I arrived in Britain, was a new Kurdish political philosophy that reflected profound changes in Apo's thinking. Like Mandela, Apo had entered prison a firebrand. Like him, he had found the isolation of a cell conducive to reflection. Apo's views softened. His commitment to armed struggle eased. So did his demand for an independent Kurdistan, replaced by a more modest proposal for a borderless, democratic confederation that reunited the four parts of Kurdistan: northern Kurdistan in Turkey, western in Syria, southern in Iraq and eastern in Iran. And in place of Apo's earlier attachment to Marxist-Leninism was a new philosophy that borrowed from socialism but also environmentalism, feminism, anarchism, communalism, social justice and self-determination.

Apo now argued that capitalism and repressive occupying states need not necessarily be overthrown. Instead, he put forward a more reasoned analysis. Any perceptive person could see that capitalism was leading humanity towards intermittent economic crisis and ecological disaster, he wrote. His new proposal was to change the system from within. The driving dynamic of capitalism – selfishness – was to be replaced with something more noble: public interest instead of self-interest; collaboration over competition; public responsibility ahead of personal reward; social good over the mere consumption of goods and services.

The emphasis was on common good and common sense, and a revitalisation of consensus and cooperation. Apo wrote that everywhere humanity was paralysed by division that, over time, had become entrenched in hierarchies: man over woman, humankind over nature, rich over poor, white over black, old over young. To base a society on exclusion in this way was a recipe for conflict and suffering, and ultimately unsustainable. Western social democracy was, in that sense, a mere halfway house on the path out of feudalism. Completing the journey required private profit to be replaced with social profit. In practical terms, that meant embracing almost all forms of progressiveness, from organic agriculture to feminism to municipal decentralisation. What's more, wrote Apo, the time was right. He was convinced the world was on the brink of a historic transformation. 'Let the guns be silenced and politics dominate,' he wrote. 'A new door is being opened from the process of armed conflict to democratisation and democratic politics. It's not the end. It's the start of a new era.'*

In prison, Apo wrote five interconnected manifestos. Two of them were extracted in booklets called *The Sociology of Freedom* and *Liberating Life: Woman's Revolution*, which were especially influential. One of Apo's sayings was: 'A country can't be free unless the women are free.' In *Liberating Life*, he went further. 'The five-thousand-year-old history of civilisation is essentially the history of the enslavement of women,' he wrote. What most men called progress, said Apo, was actually a story of humanity's gradual loss of freedom. In Neolithic times, society was matricentric, organised around mothers as 'the central life-element that both gives birth and sustains life through nurturing'. It was that system, wrote Apo, that gave us farming, villages, trade, tribes based on family and a collective social consciousness characterised by equality and freedom.

All the inequality, hierarchy, autocracy and militarism since then stemmed from the moment when man used his physical strength to usurp and denigrate woman. Man violently replaced notions of collective welfare and common ownership with private enterprise and exclusive property. Shamans and religious leaders entrenched this misogyny with faiths based on divinely ordained male dominance. Soon, all religion was based around a single male God, all states were structured around a male-dominated hierarchy, and all economies were built on

---

* https://peaceinkurdistancampaign.com/2013/03/24/ocalans-historic-newroz-2013-statement/

men's ability to earn. Sexism and power, at least as humanity had known it for five thousand years, had been more or less the same thing. What Apo called 'housewifisation' was, he said, the oldest form of slavery and 'the vilest counter-revolution ever carried out'. For the same reason, 'the solutions for all social problems in the Middle East should have women's position as focus'.*

These were the ideas that I and thousands of others devoured in our exile. They were what my comrades tried to put into practice in Rojava when Syria fell apart in civil war in 2011. I felt I had to join them. And after flying to Silemani (known as Suleimaniyah in Arabic) in northern Iraq in September 2013, then crossing into Syria, I was made the administrator of a poor neighbourhood of the city of Qamishli called Heleliyah, home to around one thousand four hundred people.

My remit was broad: to deal with people's needs. And Heleliyah needed everything: water, electricity, schools, jobs, health clinics and sanitation. We set up new direct-democratic town administrations which included Kurds, Christians, Assyrians, Arabs, Turkmens, Chechens and Armenians. We handed over the supply of water, electricity and healthcare to engineers and doctors who had not fled the war. Higher education we gave to students forced to abandon their studies in Homs, Aleppo or Damascus: they soon opened the University of Rojava, where they taught each other. We gave control of agricultural machinery to farmers. Though the anti-Kurd prejudices of the Syrian education system ensured that we lacked much

---

* http://ocalan-books.com/#/book/liberating-life-womans-revolution

professional expertise, our greatest strength, I soon discovered, was the eagerness of the people. They were delighted to volunteer to build Rojava and to run their own affairs rather than be ruled by an Arab authority from the distant south. It gave them a sense of honour and dignity.

Equally noticeable was a flowering of Kurdish culture. After centuries of hiding our songs and stories in the dark, Kurds were bursting into the street with all the colour and noise they could muster. Cultural centres sprang up all over. In every neighbourhood you would find men and women practising traditional dances and songs or giving recitals of Kurdish poems, or holding language classes where people, often for the first time in their life, could learn to read and write in their native tongue. On every street corner and in every park, everyone was talking politics with the abandon of a people arriving at a river after a long walk through the desert.

Perhaps the most dramatic change was the transformation in women's lives. Previously our women had been largely restricted to the home. Now they created women's councils, women's schools, safe-houses for women who wished to live alone, even women's driving schools and a women-only police force to investigate violence against women. All our offices were at least forty per cent staffed by women. Every leadership position was jointly held by men and women. We created new schools in which women could be educated for free. We began work on a new justice system under which child marriage was outlawed, polygamy was banned and women were equal to men in all matters.

Most significant was the creation of the women's militia, the YPJ. All over the world, soldiering was still largely men's work. The YPJ showed what folly that was. Here were self-assured, fearless, powerful women like Tolin and Medya who felt no need to abandon their femininity. Just as brotherhood described the bond between male fighters, so sisterhood expressed the loyalty between women. The YPJ showed that qualities such as endurance, courage and sacrifice could be coloured, textured and enhanced by womanliness just as well as manliness. The only difference we allowed between men and women was at the level of command. Because of men's baleful history of ordering women around, female commanders only were permitted to instruct both men and women.

I had been in my job for a few months and was closing up our community centre for lunch one day when a woman approached me barefoot and in great distress, her skin dry and lifeless, her eyes darting around the street. I showed her inside. After briefly scanning the room, the woman announced that she wanted to join the YPJ. When I asked what she knew about the YPJ and their aims, she grew suspicious. Not wishing to unnerve her further, I suggested she talk to a woman colleague of mine who worked ten minutes away.

'I can't wait that long,' said the woman. 'My family are after me. I told them I wanted to join the YPJ. They refused and instead they asked me to marry a man in exchange for my brother marrying the man's sister. I don't want to marry this man. I don't want to marry *at all*. My brother is furious. He starves me and beats me. Today he pointed a gun at my head and told me that he was going to kill me. But I still want to join the YPJ.'

I persuaded the woman to wait for my colleague, who arrived and ushered her away. I let a week pass, until I was sure the woman was no longer in Qamishli. Then I visited her family.

Her mother and brother welcomed me into a small home where garlic hung on the walls to keep scorpions away. I addressed myself to both, telling them their daughter had joined the YPJ and would not be coming home. 'It is what she wanted,' I said. 'She did not want to get married.'

There was a silence. The brother stared unhappily at the floor. After a while, the mother spoke up. 'I am happy,' she announced. 'She will be safe with them.'

I remember thinking that this was how we would build our new nation. Though everyone liked the sound of freedom, few men wanted to give up their traditional authority. But here, right in front of me, in the remaking of the relationship between a mother and a son, and a brother and a sister, was all the promise of our revolution. We were building something new, and that was difficult. If we were to succeed, it would require sitting down with families, and bosses and workers, and respectfully suggesting a path out of patriarchy and enslavement. I believed people were inherently good and that the triumph of progress over backwardness was as inevitable as time. Rojava offered proof that I might be right. To live there for those brief few months was to experience an exhilarating explosion of hope. Once the rest of humanity noticed what was happening in Rojava, I was sure we would change the world.

I still believe that now. One day, we will have a free, progressive and enlightened Kurdistan and millions around the world will follow our example, ringing the bell of liberty so loudly that it will echo through the ages. Of course, it was precisely that prospect that the jihadis wanted to destroy.

After advancing unseen to the outskirts of Qamishli in December 2013, the jihadis fired several mortars into the city one morning. I heard the impact from my office, like the sound of a giant overladen table collapsing. Running the few blocks to see the strike, I found a house had been hit. Half of it was gone and half was still standing upright, oblivious. It was a state I would come to recognise in fatally wounded people in the years to come.

Even before the Islamists attacked, people had been preparing themselves. Some families had packed up what they could and left for Turkey. Most had decided to stay, emptying the market of rice and flour and tins of oil. A few whose work required them to move in and out of the jihadis' territory – doctors and traders, mainly – could be seen in the cafés and the streets practising Islamic verses, in case they were stopped at a checkpoint.

The same day the jihadis attacked, seven of us civil administrators presented ourselves to the YPG and the YPJ for military service. We were assessed by a veteran commander of the women's militia, General Tolin. When it came to my turn, I told her that I had served in the Iranian army. She suggested the sniper unit. Because we were pressed for time, I would have just twenty-one days of basic training before being deployed to the front.

FIVE

Qamishli,

December 2013 to June 2014

Any competent soldier can learn the basics of sniping in an hour. The scope of a standard sniper rifle has a crosshair in the centre and, to the left, a curved graph with distance on the vertical axis and a flat line representing the ground on the horizontal one. You pick an average-sized man, line up his feet with the horizontal line and the top of his head with the curve, then read off the distance on the vertical axis: '2' for two hundred metres, '4' for four hundred, and so on. That's your range. To 'zero' the scope on your target, you twist a dial on the top of the scope until it is set to the required distance, between a hundred and a thousand metres. For targets more than a kilometre away, you turn the dial to a thousand metres, then use the chevrons below the crosshairs to account for gravity's pull. The top chevron is for a thousand metres, the second for a thousand one hundred, the third for a thousand two hundred, and the fourth for a thousand three hundred. You can still make shots at greater distances, but you will, to some extent, be guessing.

The marks on the horizontal crosshair are for wind. We carried pocket tables into battle on which we could read off how

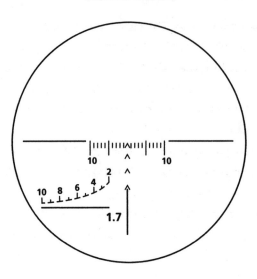

far to shoot to the left or right according to the wind's strength, its angle and the range. In the diagram, a perfect shot, taken at a range of one thousand two hundred metres in a brisk wind blowing directly from left to right, would hit the target 1.9 seconds after it was fired if the scope was zeroed to one thousand metres and the number '6' was directly over the man's head.

Every rifle has its own character and power and a sniper must learn each one's temperament. Different tools are also suited for different tasks. M16s, for which we had a handful of thermal scopes, were for night-time and close-quarters fighting. Dragunovs were for daytime and longer distances. Barrett rifles, or Zagros rifles as we called them, which were as tall as a man and mostly built from spare parts, were for day shots of a kilometre away or more.

You also need to know each gun's different firing mechanism. Any weapon can jam, and since turning on a light is a good way to get shot, we were taught to take apart and reassemble each gun in the dark. Practising with rifle parts, disassembling the mechanism and putting it together again over and over, has the added advantage of teaching you why touch is a sniper's most important sense after sight. It is through your trigger finger that you communicate with your rifle. Through it, too, you learn the different action of each weapon. The trigger of an M16 fires quickly. A Dragunov has two parts to its pull – a slow, long draw to the firing position, then a short final squeeze. A Barrett has a hair trigger. The importance of the trigger finger is why snipers go to such lengths to keep their forefingers shrouded and unbruised and why so many cut the finger off a glove to better connect with their weapon. After a while, I learned to recognise other snipers by their whiter, cleaner, smoother forefingers.

Since each gun takes a different calibre of round, a sniper needs to be familiar with their different impacts. Because M16 rounds, at 5.56mm in diameter, are much smaller, they often pass right through a target without much immediate effect. Days later, however, an M16 round can prove to be the dead-liest of all since a tight, narrow bullet hole is hardest to clean. For the same reasons, the larger 7.62mm Dragunov bullet is often fatal on impact but if a target survives, their chances of recovery are often better. Barretts fire 13mm-calibre rounds the size of a fountain pen, known as 0.50-cal because they are half an inch in diameter, which can pass through several walls and still kill you. If you are hit by a .50, survival is unlikely and is generally achieved only after the amputation of an arm or leg. Snipers generally consider Barretts and Dragunovs more honourable weapons than the M16. The first two are de-signed for clean kills. The M16 is designed to wound and trap the enemy in an impossible dilemma: rescue a fallen soldier and risk being shot himself or stay hidden and let his friend bleed out.

*

I honed my craft in eastern Rojava. For eight months I shot long-distance, alternating between a Dragunov and a Barrett. We had two frontlines, one facing south of Qamishli, the other confronting the east and the border with Iraq. On both fronts, the fighting was sporadic and conducted across open no-man's-land. Initially I was stationed at Al-Yarubiyah, the name we gave our eastern front, in the stony desert and dried-up riverbeds that lay in the shadow of Mount Shengal. We were billeted in a new five-storey administrative building. I built a hide in a toilet on the roof, hanging my Barrett from the ceiling by a strap so that it was suspended in the air and pointed through the window at the ISIS positions about a kilometre and a half away.

During my first few days on the front, the constant *fzzz* of bullets overhead made me tense up and blink. Every now and then ISIS would start up a mortar barrage and I would grab my rifle and run down a floor inside the building. Even when I had time to fire, I mostly missed. If I was startled during my shot, as often happened, the bullet would veer wide to the left. A rushed shot meant it skewed right.

I soon learned not to blink or flinch. But mastering my breathing took longer. As you prepare to shoot, your breaths must be almost like meditation. You start with a chest full of air. You breathe out half of it as you line up your sights on your target. At that point, you pause for up to six seconds. Too much air and you'll shoot high. Too little and you'll tip forward and the bullet will go low. The idea is to slow your heart and blood so that nothing, not even your pulse, shakes your aim. For the same reason, you hold the rifle to your bones, not your flesh. Through those five or six long, deep, calm seconds, you stay focused on the target, squeezing your trigger. You fire almost without realising. The slower and stiller you are, the truer the bullet leaves the barrel.

I started hitting the enemy after a week or so. From my position on the roof I could see a hospital building inside Iraq where ISIS had placed a tripod-mounted Dushka heavy machine gun. A Dushka could shoot through several buildings and still kill one of ours. If my enduring mission was to stop the ISIS attacks, my daily preoccupation was taking down the Dushka operator. Each morning I would wait for the Dushka to open up, after which I would return fire and shut him down. I fired at that gun for weeks. I must have hit more than a dozen men behind it.

I had other targets, too. One time, during an ISIS advance, I fired more than twenty times at an ISIS pickup that was dashing back and forth along a road more than a kilometre away, only for an American jet to sweep in, fire a rocket and send the vehicle flying through the air as though it were a stone skipping across a pond. That was the first I knew that the US was supporting us with air attacks. I remember being amazed by how quiet that distant scene was.

As I became more experienced, I realised that sniping was as much about human observation as shooting skill. Through the scope, I learned to be able to size up my enemy at a glance: the way he held himself, the way he walked, whether he was confident with his rifle, whether he was careful with his approach, how long his beard was. If I caught a glimpse of someone walking loosely, with his hands hanging down by his knees and his shoulders collapsed – someone who was weak and without purpose or hope – I knew that was someone who was going to make a mistake, and that our advancing team should direct their initial attack at his position. On the other hand, a jihadi who had real purpose, who moved like a mouse, popping up and down, and checking all around himself, was going to be much harder to shoot. But he was also more likely to be someone of stature, and therefore a more important target.

When I was going after a truly high-value target such as another sniper or a high-ranking officer, I would try to create a portrait of my target: who he was, how he behaved, how old he was, what time he woke up, whether he preferred the cold of the morning or the heat of the day. From these studies, it was possible to make some predictions about where and when my enemy would show himself and how to position myself to take advantage. It required total concentration. I had to observe all the information I could, analyse it in an instant, and draw a conclusion about where to target and when.

My enemies, who knew I was watching them, often tried to frustrate my observations. They would stay hidden, erect curtains and build corridors through houses, firing through holes in the walls. It was like boxing. You sized up your opponent, tried to hold for your opportunity, and eventually took your shot. Many times I had to go by what I heard, not what I could see. On more than one occasion my target looked right at me and even waved at me. Some played games, running into view, then stopping for a split second, then running on again. Once, for days, I tried to shoot a motorbiker who was crossing a street in front of me about seven hundred metres away. I could hear him coming from the sound of his revving engine, then he would burst across the street and I would fire – once, twice – and he'd be gone, tooting his horn as if to say: 'You missed! I am still alive!'

Often the idea behind these games was to tempt me into giving away my position by firing. They weren't without risk for the players: I once hit a man running across a street from eight hundred metres away. Another ISIS tactic was to try to spook us by enforcing a silence. At those times, every sound – the wind blowing through my firing hole, shaking the corrugated roof and the clothes on a washing line – would become so loud. The idea was to give us too much time to think. What were they doing? How come I couldn't hear them? Were they going to attack?

Since our enemy was also watching us, we practised our own manipulations and deceptions. We dug holes in walls through which to shoot, then dug new ones in less likely positions – close to the ceiling or hidden by a shadow – to fool ISIS into targeting the unmanned ones. We dampened our holes with water so that our shots didn't kick up dust and reveal our positions. We switched lights on and off in places we didn't use. We left signs of movement in corridors through which we never passed. We even used mannequins to confuse the enemy. Often I found I had most success in lining up a shot, then persuading my enemy to walk into it by pretending I was somewhere else. I'd take down one man, then wait for his friend to run out, too.

After a few months, I found that my instincts had augmented and sharpened. I acquired the ability to judge distances to within a few metres without the aid of a scope. I learned to distinguish the different sounds, sights and trajectories of different bullets. I found enemies with my eyes, my ears and even my nose. I also developed my own technique for scanning an area, standing square on to the range and closing my eyes, then opening them again, then closing, then opening. Repeated three or four times, I found this camera-shutter technique would print an image on my mind which I could then examine at leisure for anything unusual, almost as though I was looking at a picture in my hands.

As my technique improved and my knowledge expanded, I felt something swell inside me. Not quite confidence, nor hope, nor will, though it contained shades of all three. Mostly I felt I was uncovering a long-buried instinct for survival. Somehow, I knew I possessed the ability to endure and overcome. It was there in how I tuned in to the moment, how I learned to listen to my intuition. It was about accepting the battle as inescapable and entering it with the calm trust that you will somehow sense what to do and how to react. This is the peace in war.

To be a good sniper, of course, you need to come to terms with the idea of taking human life. When I thought of blood and killing, my mind always went back to my village in East Kurdistan and my mother showing me how to dispatch a chicken as a boy. It was a mess. Once I began shooting, I was surprised how clean it could be. Soldiers on the ground have to confront the hot intimacy of death. Snipers dispatch in cold blood, often silently and without sensation.

After five months of taking long shots and watching distant guns fall silent, the day finally came when I saw it all. I was hiding with an attack team in a village house on the eastern front, watching a second village less than two kilometres away where ISIS had a position. We could see them moving around their base, positioning sandbags and moving rocks for cover.

'They're using a bulldozer,' said one of my team, looking through binoculars at a plume of black smoke coming from the village. 'They're breaking down houses and turning the rubble into fortifications.'

That was the signal for the team to start shooting. It was unlikely that they would hit much at that range but at least they could harass the enemy. As they did so, I crept forward on my elbows, sweating in the summer heat, until I guessed I was within range. Dragging my Barrett into position, I checked the distance through the scope: one thousand and five metres.

I zeroed the scope to a thousand metres and settled in to watch. I could see two ISIS fighters, one skinny and one big. They were heaving the three legs of a heavy Dushka into position to fire at us. I couldn't allow that. The bigger fighter walked away, apparently to retrieve something. When he turned around and walked back towards me, I thought to myself: *This is my guy. I might miss the skinny one. This bigger man is the guy.*

I followed him through the scope, my crosshairs on his chest. He had a rifle with him. At one point, he bent over the Dushka, manoeuvring it to target us.

I exhaled.

One . . .

Two . . .

I didn't hear the shot. I barely noticed the kick. But as if I were watching a silent movie, I saw that big man knocked right into the air, then fly four or five metres back, all the way into the backyard of a house behind him. I saw the whole thing. I still see it now.

SIX

Kobani,

October 2014

The night after my briefing from Tolin, we set out to cross the ISIS frontline. For five hours we crawled silently on the ground and ducked between the houses, following a guide who was equipped with one of our few night-vision scopes. As we approached ISIS' positions, we could hear them in houses on either side of us. We tried to move slowly and carefully to avoid making noise but we also had to cross before the sun came up and revealed us to the enemy. Twice we had to back-track after nearly walking into a jihadi base. Several times we had to wait for their sentries to pass. Finally, we passed the last house on the outskirts of town and sprinted for cover in the fields beyond.

Just before dawn, we found an abandoned village on a hill twelve kilometres inside ISIS territory in which we hoped to hide ourselves without being discovered. Below us, about six hundred metres away, was the main road from Kobani to Aleppo. All day we watched the jihadis drive up and down in their pickups and motorbikes, so close I could distinguish them by the length of their beards. But attacking them when they were together would have meant a very quick death. Our mission was to stay concealed and send out small teams of two or three on sabotage and assassination missions several kilometres away from where we were hiding.

For two weeks, we crawled in the dirt, sweating through the day and freezing all night. Within a few days, everyone was sick with flu and fever. But we also had success. A de-mining team that was part of our group rewired an old device, then detonated it under one of their pickups. When the jihadis arrived to investigate, we killed all four of them, then hid their bodies to confuse the Islamists further. We shot another two on a motorbike, then stowed their bodies and their bike under a bridge. We would hear the shouts of confusion as their friends arrived to find them dead so far from the frontline.

One day, all seventy of us were hiding in the village when a BMW camouflaged with mud sped in from the countryside and skidded to a halt under a large mulberry tree perhaps five metres in front of us. Inside were two ISIS fighters, dressed in black with long beards. They stepped out of the car and began scanning the sky. Overhead, we could hear one of the two American fighter jets which had begun patrolling the skies above Kobani in the past week.

The way we were positioned, we were already surrounding the car. We were deliberating whether or not to shoot, and give away our position, when a shot rang out from one of our units – and after that, we all opened up. One of the jihadis died instantly: he turned out to be a general with valuable information on a memory stick in his pocket. The driver, a tiny man, scurried behind a small stone wall, then ran into a house behind it shouting, 'Surrender if you want to live!' There were seventeen volunteers inside that house waiting for him, their guns levelled at the door. That tiny man flew back out of the house and landed in the garden.

After two weeks of harassing, sabotaging and killing as deep as twenty kilometres behind ISIS' frontline, our last mission was to inflict a final humiliation on the Islamists by heading back to Kobani and, coordinating with comrades inside the town, attacking them from behind as our other forces harassed them from the front. We moved silently in three teams – one to my left, one to my right and my team in the centre – radioing ahead to our forces inside Kobani to fire so as to distract the jihadis, allowing us to surprise them from behind.

After four hours, shortly after 1 a.m. we found ourselves walking by moonlight through the olive farms and farmhouses below Mistenur Hill. This was the strategic gateway to Kobani. As we rounded a cluster of boulders on its lower slopes, we could see the entire town before us. Descending into the streets again felt like stepping out into the ocean. The sound of gunfire up ahead – Kalashnikovs, Dushkas, RPGs – became constant. Bullets began splitting the air over our heads. Black smoke soon enveloped us, choking us but covering our advance. Deeper and deeper we marched. On the right, one of our units came across a house of jihadis and killed six of them. On the left, there was another firefight, with the same result. All of a sudden the Islamists seemed to realise they were being encircled. We heard shouts of '*Allahu Akbar*'. For a few minutes, they fought intensely. Three of our volunteers were injured but we returned fire and killed five of them. After that, the remaining Islamists seemed to lose heart. The gunfire stopped. As we walked on, moving house to house, we found empty buildings and abandoned trenches.

Shortly before dawn, we crossed back over our lines. In the first position we came to, we found two YPJ fighters facing us.

These two women were holed up together in a house, alone, almost out of ammunition, their radio dead and their eyes red from exhaustion. They said they had been there for four days, part of a thin line holding out against attacks that could last seven hours at a time. Of our original force of four hundred and fifty, the two women said scores, possibly more than a hundred, had died in the days we had been away. On either side of them, they knew of only seven survivors. We relieved them, pulling desks and refrigerators across the doors and mining the front garden. And almost without anyone noticing, the smoke lifted and the light of morning broke over Kobani.

Before us lay our new frontline, one block further south than when I had arrived. I was free to walk north through the streets. Everywhere my comrades were preparing new defences, digging trenches, filling sandbags and pillows, knocking new firing holes in the houses. It was hard not to feel a small sense of triumph. A few days earlier, Turkish President Recep Tayyip Erdoğan had predicted that Kobani would fall to ISIS within hours. We had proved him wrong. Though we had gained just one street, we had stopped them and turned them around. Possibility rippled through our people like a wind through grass. If we had done it once, we could do it again.

All the time I was behind enemy lines, I had been without a sniper's rifle. The morning I crossed back over, I tried to find my way to the snipers' base to equip myself. That was when I met the others.

The first I encountered was Herdem. I was in the street talking with Tolin when he strode up and interrupted. 'Walk out of the back of that building,' he said to me, pointing to a ruined house across the street, 'turn to the right and there is a burned-out black van parked in front of a house. That's where we have our headquarters. I'll see you there.' That was Herdem's way of saying hello.

I had heard of Herdem before I arrived. He had been in Kobani since the start of the war and had become something of a legend. In the months ahead, a Turkish photographer from a French news agency would take a series of portraits of him crouching in the ruins of the city, his black beanie pulled down low over his forehead, his black Dragunov slung across his back. The images would become famous, turning Herdem into a latter-day Che Guevara, a symbol of freedom to millions. The pictures captured Herdem as I knew him: sharp, intense, silent and alone. In the years since, other photographs have emerged of a younger man laughing in a meadow of flowers, shaking the hand of a general or playing a lyre on a rooftop, his Dragunov lying next to him on the tiles. I'd like to have met that other Herdem. The one I knew fought every hour of every day.

I followed Herdem's directions to the snipers' base, which turned out to be an equipment store for the sharp-shooters of both the YPG and YPJ. There I met a broad-shouldered woman with her black hair tied in a ponytail and a pronounced cow-lick that was turning grey. She introduced herself as Yildiz, commander of the YPJ's snipers. If Herdem was gruff and monosyllabic, Yildiz was the opposite. She immediately engaged me in a discussion on the tactics of building bases, arguing that when we were advancing there wasn't always time to sandbag a nest. 'Just throw a few empty sandbags on yourself and hide in the rubble,' she said. 'It's much smarter. People get stuck into one way of doing things and we need to remember always to be flexible.'

As the leaders of our snipers, Herdem and Yildiz made a

point of visiting their shooters on the frontline. Herdem would generally stick to issuing commands. Yildiz always seemed like she was dropping in for a chat. One day she found me only a few hundred metres from the enemy, reached up to me with a glass of hot black tea and suddenly started talking about the art of making infusions, how there were different teas with different tastes and strengths and colours, and how it made such a difference whether you used an electric kettle or a smoky wood fire and whether the water was from a tap or fresh from a spring. I used to relish these monologues – about tea or the value of a good pair of combat trousers or the beauty and peace of a morning fog. They were diverting and refreshing and, for the briefest of moments, I was transported to another time and place. But with Yildiz, there was always a lesson for the present. When I laughed and complimented her on how much she knew about tea, Yildiz replied that the point was that the harder and more creatively you worked for it, the better the tea. It was the same with defending Kobani, she said. The more care you took, the more effort you made, the better the result.

I understood that Yildiz's chatter was also her attempt to distract us. There were a number of subjects no sniper would ever discuss. We never talked about the fragility of our endeavour, for instance. Eight months of fighting had taught us all that there was no meritocracy in war. On the days when death came and snatched a life to the left of you and another few to the right, it was tempting to imagine it was working to a scheme, the way a sculptor whittles away the extraneous and leaves only the fine and necessary. But that was a delusion. I had seen the best warriors fall in the first shots of battle. I had seen the least experienced pass through the fiercest fights unscathed. Death could be a brave sacrifice or a lowly accident. Alexander the Great conquered most of the world only to be bitten by a malarial mosquito. A day's drive west of Rojava was the Saleph river in which Holy Roman Emperor Frederick Barbarossa died, an old man who had won innumerable battles dragged under the water by the weight of his own chain mail. There was no predictability to war, no logic to death, and no arguing with any of it. Death took, tirelessly and carelessly. You couldn't explain it, and to discuss it was pointless. You could only accept it.

The war required us to live with unpredictability. Faced with chaos, the only real plan is to have no plan. Fear is what you don't know, whether it's war or ISIS or death, and by Kobani we were acquainted well enough with all three not to be surprised by any of them. Practising, learning, adapting, the craft of life and death – that was how you found purpose and focus.

Maybe our facility for calm concentration was one reason why the five of us – Hayri, Herdem, Yildiz, Nasrin and I – had survived long enough to find ourselves in the same place at the same time. It was certainly true that when we were together there was a peace to our group. We couldn't afford a noisy mind. By the nature of the work, we were quiet loners. Others confronted the enemy face to face. We floated above, moving from unit to unit and commander to commander. They fired as they had to. We fired when we chose to. We depended almost entirely on ourselves – and the experience set us apart. We didn't share. It was months before I learned that Yildiz was originally from North Kurdistan and had been in the movement for years. So at home did Herdem seem in Kobani that it was only years later that I read that he didn't come from the city but a small village high up in the mountains on the border between Iran and Turkey.

As for Nasrin, I never learned anything about her life before the war. Nasrin was blue-eyed, pale-skinned and short, with a round face marked by sharp wrinkles around her eyes. She always wore a red *keffiyeh* – a headscarf – blue jeans and a bulky military sweater. Other than that, there was just her commitment and the unspoken measure we had of each other, a bond somehow stronger because we exchanged so few words. She would never talk about what happened at the front or what she had seen or the three times she was wounded, and I never once heard her mention her kills. Those who did speak about killing were generally looking for acceptance or credit. I preferred Nasrin's silent capability. You could see she had the will. Anything she did, even offering you a cup of tea so the handle faced you, she did with decency and care.

We had two snipers with us who were not fit to fight, one so depressed he couldn't talk, another, an eighteen-year-old, who complained all the time that he was never sent to the front. I had no time for either. But Nasrin would listen to them like a mother. When I was with her, the two of us often sat in silence, content to be in the company of a comrade who understood. If we spoke, it was to swap tactics or techniques or tips for equipment maintenance. For months, the most I heard her say was that first day at the base when I selected a Dragunov from the rack and she complimented me on my choice, saying the weapon was a favourite of hers as the scope was extremely precise. Everything else – the shots we had made, the expression on an enemy's face as you pulled the trigger, the youth of some of those we had to take down – we left unsaid.

Perhaps the gentlest among us was Hayri. Hayri had arrived in Kobani with Nasrin and like Yildiz he was from North Kurdistan, though I never knew precisely where. He had a black-and-white scarf which he always wore. I had a similar one in my pack, and Hayri's way of introducing himself was to take the loose threads hanging from mine and say, 'You're knotting these up wrong. You need to make them thinner. Then they'll look better.' Then, to show me, he began twisting the threads around each other and tying them.

'It's quicker my way,' I said.

'But not as pretty,' he replied, smiling.

Other people would tell me Hayri was a great sniper, a person of discipline and character. Like Nasrin, he never talked about the war or how he handled it. If anyone asked, Hayri would just smile and stare off into the distance. I think, like all of us, he thought killing was abhorrent. But faced with the choice we all faced, us or them, Hayri had made his peace with it. He didn't need to explain or justify. He took responsibility for what he was doing. And if there was death and dying all around, to Hayri that made it even more important that two comrades who were alive and well greeted each other and shared a moment in each other's company. Don't let death consume you, he was saying. Remember life.

SEVEN

Sardasht,
1983–1997

I was born in the autumn of 1983 in Sardasht, a small town next to a hill spring in northern Iran, below the mountains where the borders of Iran, Iraq and Turkey converge. My father, mother, two sisters and I lived in the upper part of town, on a road leading out into the fields and towards the peaks. The walls of our house were made of stone and mud, the floors were cement and our roof was tin. We had a toilet, a bath-room and a kitchen downstairs and, upstairs, two bedrooms, one for my parents, and one for me and my sisters. We slept on the floor under blankets made by my mother. We ate rice, tomatoes, aubergines, soup, bread, salad and fried potatoes and, once a week, chicken or goat or trout from the river. My mother's pride was an oil-heated hot-water tank, big enough for a shower. Still, when the snow came in winter we would freeze, while in summer the house was like an oven. Then we would stretch out on the roof at night and fall asleep watching the stars in the cool breeze.

Most of the families in our street traced their origins back thousands of years to the people who first settled the lush valleys at the foot of the Zagros mountains. For centuries, they had tended mountain vineyards producing Sardasht's famous black grapes, which they ate fresh or turned furtively into strong, sweet wine. By the time I was born, several thousand families had abandoned the fields for the town, where the men found work as shopkeepers, bureaucrats or book-keepers, and the women worked as nurses, seamstresses or teachers.

My father was a trader, travelling to and from Iraq, returning with cheap Chinese tea sets, European car parts and American military-surplus jackets. He liked to keep up with technology. We were among the first people we knew to have a telephone. I remember my sisters and I waiting in the kitchen for it to ring, arguing over who was going to pick up – though, of course, since almost no one else had a phone, we sometimes waited for weeks. We were also the first in our street to have a television. My mother, who made traditional clothes and wedding dresses for the neighbourhood, stitched a cotton shawl to hang over the screen to keep the dust at bay. At weekends, the entire street would crowd into our house and watch black-and-white images of Iranian newsreaders and Japanese cartoons. My favourite show was *The Wonderful Adventures of Nils*, about a miniature boy brought up on a farm who hitches a ride on the back of a white goose and is taken on a grand tour of Sweden. What I loved about it was how at first Nils is punished for his naughtiness but, in the end, his pure spirit is celebrated.

Even in the city, the families stayed close to the land. Before he became a trader, my father had been a vegetable grower. He still kept a plot outside town and in our backyard, like most of our neighbours, we grew lilies and flame nettles and towering elephant ears and sharp, spiky mother-in-law's tongue. In spring, everyone would sandbag their doors against the flash floods which would roar down from the mountains and funnel through the streets, ripping up the asphalt and burying it under avalanches of mud. In the summer, people would head out to the fields, where they would pick fruit and vegetables and lay them on rugs for a picnic. One of my earliest memories is of my mother's friends taking me out to the countryside on their backs and passing me around, fussing over whether I was chubby enough.

As a young boy, the countryside was my playground. In the winter, the rivers would freeze and my friends and I would skate, using shoes whose rubber soles we made as smooth as river pebbles by rubbing them on our mothers' iron stoves. In spring I would hunt for tiny birds which I would knock off their perches with a catapult I made from the tongue of a shoe tied to a pair of washing-up gloves, then hurry over to my aunt's, who would fry them whole, ten to a pan. I became quite the shot. Later, of course, my marksmanship would prove useful. But as a boy my mother was always scolding me for breaking neighbours' windows and climbing onto their roofs. Come the long weekends of summer, however, she and my father were happy for my friends and I to head off into the country, where we walked for hours through vineyards and orchards of figs, pears and plums, on through a deep, cool oak forest until we reached a waterfall at whose edge we would sit and eat watermelon. Sometimes we would jump in. Sometimes we would fish. I loved sinking my feet into the cold, clear water. It washed away the city. It felt like freedom.

When I look back now, though my childhood was mostly one of idyllic innocence, I think I was always aware of a looming malevolence that might crush us all at any moment. I probably have Saddam Hussein to thank for that. Sardasht was only four hours' walk from the Iraqi border. From the day Iran began shelling Kurdish villages over the frontier in 1980 in response to an Iraqi invasion further south, my father had been expecting the Iraqis to retaliate. He carved out a shelter deep in the rock beneath our front yard. Some of the neighbours laughed at this barely literate man and his bunker. They laughed harder still when, during the times that he sensed trouble, he herded us underground with a small oil torch and a pile of towels which he would dip in a bucket of water and hand to my sisters and I to hold over our mouths and noses.

But on 28 June 1987, when I was three, the sirens sounded, the gas fell and that evening my father, mother, two sisters and I emerged from our shelter to discover that in and around the bazaar one hundred and thirty people had died screaming and vomiting, six hundred and fifty had lost their faces or entire sides of their bodies and eight thousand were poisoned, including my uncle Fouad, who wheezed like a harmonica for the rest of his life. To the world, the Iranian government made much of the attack, demonising Saddam, forcing the last of his Western friends to desert him and making him pay Tehran billions of barrels of oil in compensation. But in Sardasht, we never saw any of it. The regime in Iran, we figured, hated Kurds as much as their neighbours in Iraq, Turkey or Syria.

The story of my people is filled with bitter ironies like these. The Kurds are one of the world's oldest peoples and, as pioneers of agriculture, were once among its most advanced. Though the rest of humanity now largely overlooks how it was Kurds who were among the first to create a civilisation, the evidence is there. In 1995, German archaeologists excavated a temple discovered by a Kurdish shepherd at Göbekli Tepe in northern Kurdistan. They found a structure flanked by twenty-ton stone pillars carved with bulls, foxes and cranes, which they dated to 11,000 BCE. At the end of the last Ice Age, when most human beings were still wearing furs and living in caves, and a full eight and a half thousand years before the erection of Stonehenge or the pyramids at Giza, my ancestors were living together as shamans, artists, farmers and engineers.

That our ancestors picked this spot to cultivate always struck me as bull-headed. To live in the mountains was to risk your animals freezing in winter and your crops being washed away by the spring floods, while to live on the plains was to invite them to wither and die in summer droughts. But if the great strength of the Kurds was their resilience, their great blight has been the greed and laziness of others who, as far back as anyone can remember, wanted our farms and markets for themselves.

For the last few millennia, our people have been conquered by a succession of outsiders. First Persians, then Seleucids, Romans, Daylamites, Islamists, Turks, Mongols, Safavids, Afsharids, Zands, Qajars, Ottomans, then finally the British and the French. The first Kurdish uprising happened in 838. There have been twenty-six since. Despite possessing our own language and culture and a population of forty-five million – ranking us alongside Spain, Argentina and Uganda as the thirtieth most populous nation in the world – today our people and our nation still pass unrecognised as either, split between what others call southern Turkey, northern Syria, northern Iraq and northwestern Iran. In each of these misnamed, amputated limbs Kurds are repressed. Intermittent bans outlaw our language, dress, folklore, our names and, in Turkey, even the words 'Kurd', 'Kurdistan' and 'Kurdish' (we are, instead, 'mountain Turks'). Our struggle has also been alternately embraced and betrayed by the wider world. The Allies promised to create Kurdistan after the end of World War I and the dissolution of the Ottoman Empire, only to allow Turkey to block it.

Britain backed the Kurds when we declared the independence
of the Republic of Ararat in eastern Turkey in 1927, then let
the Turks reconquer it in 1930. When Kurds in Turkey formed
the militant Kurdish Workers Party (PKK) in 1978, Turkey
persuaded the world to classify it as a terrorist group. After the
end of the Gulf War in 1991, the US and others urged the
Kurds to rise up against Saddam (who had killed one hundred
and eighty-two thousand Kurds in the 1980s), then abandoned
us when we did so and let twenty thousand refugees who fled
die of cold and exhaustion. Two years later, the world stood by
when Turkish death squads killed a further three thousand two
hundred Kurds and Assyrians.

With our obstinate farmers' blood, we have never given up.
When I was young, my mother would tell me the legend of
Kawa, the blacksmith, who was said to have come from a small
nameless town tucked into the folds of the Zagros mountains.
Above the town was an enormous castle with tall turrets cut out
of the mountain rock and gates carved in the shape of winged
warriors. There lived a cruel Assyrian king, Dehak, who had
been possessed by an evil spirit, Ahriman. Until Dehak's
time, people had only eaten bread, herbs, fruit and nuts. But
Ahriman, who had disguised himself as a cook, fed the king the
flesh of animals.

One day, Ahriman kissed Dehak on his shoulders, there was
a flash of light and two giant black snakes sprouted above his
arms. The only way Dehak could assuage the snakes' hunger
was feeding them the brains of young boys and girls. From then
on, the townspeople were forced to make regular sacrifices of
their children, killing them two at a time and delivering their
brains to the castle in a walnut-wood bucket.

With the advent of this great evil, darkness fell on the land.
Crops, trees and flowers withered. Peacocks, partridges and

eagles left. None felt the pain of Dehak's rule more than Kawa and his wife, who gave up sixteen of their children. When Kawa and his wife were told to give up their seventeenth and last, Kawa sent his surviving daughter to a valley far away and delivered instead the brain of a sheep to Dehak. The king didn't notice the deception, the other townsfolk copied Kawa, and soon there were hundreds of children living secretly in the mountains. Eventually, Kawa led the children in a rebellion, they stormed Dehak's castle and Kawa killed Dehak with his blacksmith's hammer. Dehak, Ahriman and the possessive serpents of greed were gone. The next day, the sun rose once more, flowers bloomed, trees blossomed and the animals returned. To this day every spring equinox, Kurds celebrate Newroz, or 'New Day', and the destiny that it promises: that after a long, dark night of repression, the bright day of freedom will dawn.

Of course, a key element of that story – that the first fighter in Kawa's army was a girl – is *haram* (forbidden by Islamic law) in much of the present-day Middle East. In Iran's case, when Ayatollah Khomeini seized power in Tehran in 1979, his regime enshrined misogyny in law. God was a man, as was the Prophet, and that, said our new leaders, gave men a divine right to subjugate women. Men could have up to four wives and marry girls as young as nine. But women couldn't work, bear witness, divorce or, should a man divorce them, expect custody of their children. These laws were enforced by a male-only religious order and a male-only judiciary, both of which equated feminism and femininity with indecency.

The Kurds have women like my mother to thank that such bone-headedness never conquered our people. She was kind and honest, and a caring and loving mother. But as a wife, she refused to submit to my father or defer to his will, as the Iranian state and traditional patriarchy demanded. My parents fought constantly. My father insisted that my mother recognise him as the head of the family and herself as family property. My mother insisted she was an independent woman who required no man's permission to do what she wanted, go where she liked and say what she thought. Her honour and integrity were inseparable from her freedom, she said. These were not qualities to be found in meekly obeying a husband or taking note of neighbours' gossip. More than once, the two of them came to blows.

A few men in Sardasht despised my mother for her independence. Many others, and almost all the women, admired her for what, under Iranian law, was close to revolutionary courage. People would talk about how clean her spirit was and how she carried herself with dignity. She was a huge influence on anyone who knew her including, eventually, my father. As her son, I hated it when my parents fought. But I also understood that my mother was holding fast to her beliefs and self-respect. Today I can see that the life I chose had everything to do with the tenacity and dignity she showed me as a boy.

I had my own battles at school. At seven, I was suddenly in a world where even the most basic things such as bread or water or home had a new Farsi name. I often couldn't understand a word that my Iranian teachers said. Nor could I read the new Arabic alphabet. Even my people's ancient story was replaced with the eleven-year footnote of history that was the story of Iran since the 1979 revolution. To me, school felt like a conspiracy designed to favour the Iranian boys and girls, who were forever one step ahead, and to guarantee the disappointment of my father, who had bought me new shoes and clothes for my classes. The injustice of it gave me a headache. I spent my days praying for snowstorms to close the school. My mother, who was illiterate, valued education but shared my suspicion of Iran's version of it, and her example gave me the strength to endure the unfairness of it. On weekends or during the holidays I began disappearing to the villages outside the city. Unsurprisingly, I was made to repeat my first year. Even today I have trouble with basic mathematics and spelling.

Outside school, my mother took a fierce interest in every aspect of my development. If she didn't like the look of a neighbour's family, she would ban me from seeing their children. One day, when I was eleven, I got into a fight at school with a boy called Shina who was two years older than me. When I arrived home with a bleeding nose, my mother asked me what had happened, then marched me round to the boy's house to confront his mother. When the woman emerged, however, it turned out she and my mother were old friends from the same village and had played together as girls. I was impressed when the other woman slapped Shina across the mouth, splitting his lip. Then, to our mutual disgust, Shina and I were made to hug each other. Much to our surprise, we quickly became good friends.

One of the things Shina and I agreed on was how much we hated the religious leaders who even we boys could see were using faith to terrorise people. My family was especially sceptical of Iran's theocracy. When the weather was fine, my father and his friends would take me for barbecues. The men would build a big fire and cook chicken and fish and drink wine. One time, as a young teenager, I was fasting for Ramadan and my uncles, who saw no connection between holiness and hunger, were having another feast. 'Eat!' they told me. When I declined, they held me down and, laughing, forced a piece of chicken into my mouth. After that, they gave me a glass of 'grape juice'.

In time, Ramadan barbecues became a family ritual. Pious neighbours objected, which was their right, but we felt they were missing the point. It wasn't that we didn't believe in anything. We believed in our land. We were inspired by Nature's gifts and celebrated what it gave us. We were happy in our place. That was our faith. We would say that you could betray your land or even leave it, but it would never betray or leave you.

Matters came to a head for me around the age of fourteen. The older I became, the clearer I could see the discrimination and injustice around me. I started taking notice of how many soldiers the Iranian regime had stationed in our streets. Why did our own government feel the need constantly to check our identity? Why did they require tanks to face us? Why did they plaster Sardasht with photographs of dead Iranian soldiers, killed as they tried to crush our people's dissent? I wasn't sleeping well and getting into fights. Despite my agnosticism, my mother told me that she had heard that there were some verses in the Koran that calmed the nerves and she suggested I take up prayer. So I learned one *hadith* and practised it over and over every night before I went to bed. Unfortunately, the exercise only deepened my distress. *I'm saying my prayers in Arabic,* I thought. *But I'm Kurdish. Why should I denounce my language? What God is this, if he can only understand Arabic? If this God doesn't like Kurdish, then this Kurd doesn't like this God.*

Doubt about the state was one thing. But to deny God was a huge leap. For two months I was caught between my anger and a suspicion that I would burn in hell. I felt there was something inside me – not the devil exactly, but a restlessness, an undeniable sense of self-determination. For weeks, I felt torn. I was just a small boy from a small mountain city and I was blaspheming before the Almighty. Why hadn't I thought it through?

Then one day, hiking in the mountains, all my doubts vanished. *There is no God*, I heard myself say. *Religion is illusion. The mountains and the trees, the eagles and the rivers – they are the real peace and harmony. Why look for anything more?*

It's probably no coincidence that around the same age I started showing an interest in politics. Shina, who was sixteen by then, was already a member of an underground left-wing Kurdish nationalist party called Komala. He would spend his free time distributing socialist pamphlets critical of the regime. I began to read the articles, which were about social injustice, colonisation and Kurdish culture and how we were third-class citizens in our homeland, starved by an invader state of jobs, electricity, hospitals and roads. Often the pamphlets contained wrenching memorials to Kurds who had died in prison or been hanged.

The words had a profound effect on me. I began joining Shina on his subversive newspaper round every month, venturing out after dark with the new issue, throwing it over walls into people's gardens and tucking it inside their doors. To be caught handing out anti-state publications would mean a lengthy spell in prison or worse, so Shina devised a system whereby he was the only party member I knew and he was the only person who knew of me. With my experience now, I can see that what he created was an archetypal dissident cell.

At the time, Komala's influence was spreading and the authorities were beginning to feel it. One day, we were all ushered into Sardasht's central square and told we had been gathered to witness a hanging. Officially, the condemned man was said to have killed his friend in an accident, dropping something on his head when they were drinking. The truth, people whispered, was that he was a Komala activist like Shina and me.

The guy was young, maybe twenty-eight or so, and they had him stand on a small table in front of a crowd of thousands. I saw his mother, begging the authorities and being restrained by the guards. When they put the rope around his neck, the woman broke free and ran to her son, trying to save him, but they threw her to the ground and held her there. She screamed. Her voice was still echoing around the mountains when they pushed her son off the table. He struggled, then went quiet. But when they took him down, he was still alive. Twice more they strung him back up. Twice more they brought him down again only to find he was still breathing. Finally, they just left him hanging there.

It seems so clear now that the authorities' purpose was to terrify us. At the time, all I could feel was disgust. It was a show, a filthy circus. They had brought us together to watch somebody's death, and we had stood there and seen it. It was sickening. And somehow, just by watching, they made us complicit.

I can still feel the anger and shame that grew in me as I walked home. Nobody had the right to take somebody's life to demonstrate the power of the state. Why did we have to fear them? Why punish a man for calling for his freedom? How could these people call themselves pious? How could they demand our respect and obedience when they did something so vile and sordid? The Iranian regime had managed to provoke a reaction in me that was the precise opposite of what they intended. And I have pursued my freedom ever since.

EIGHT

Kobani,

October 2014

The day after I met Herdem, he returned to the snipers' base to find me. 'We're going to the southern front, close to where you crossed back into Kobani,' he announced. 'I hear you've been shooting long-range.' He handed me a Barrett. 'Be careful,' he said. 'There's only one. We had to make the scope ourselves from parts.'

I jumped into Herdem's small van and we drove south for a few blocks. Autumn was now upon us, it was freezing, and Herdem was wearing a black woollen beanie. As we turned a corner, Herdem started bobbing his head up and down, looking sharply left and right. He reminded me of a character in a film I had seen once.

'You look like a car thief,' I laughed.

Herdem regarded me seriously. 'You can get shot here,' he said. 'A bullet can come from anywhere. Positions change. Buildings disappear. You go for a piss, come back and everything's different. You have no idea where you are or where the enemy is.'

I should have paid more attention.

*

Herdem dropped me at a three-storey house on our southern frontline, one of ten buildings we held there. Unlike the built-up areas that formed most of our territory, buildings in the southern part of Kobani were spread out, with open space between them. Our front formed a slow curve from east to west, strung between the buildings we held. The house I now entered was in the middle of a street, with a garden in front and a clear view of the enemy's lines which could be as close as the house across the street or as much as a mile away. Inside my new base were seven comrades led by a YPJ commander called Viyan. I made my introductions, then headed for the roof.

In the distance, I could see a small village on the edge of the city occupied by ISIS. Next to it was a graveyard. To its right was the main road to Aleppo. To its left was Mistenur Hill. It was a cold and sunny day, clear enough that I could see that some of the village houses had gardens. One was bordered by a wall that looked strange, as though it were somehow too long. I studied it through my scope. Eventually I realised that the enemy had extended the wall by adding a beige curtain. It was just within range but it was hard to see what I would be shooting at.

There were other problems with my position. I was the only sniper on this part of the front, covering one hundred and fifty people, but from my vantage I could only fire across about a third of our line. The whole set-up was frustrating. When Herdem came back after two days, I told him I needed coffee, and action. 'It's boring,' I told him. 'There's some movement. Maybe a guy running from time to time. But it's too far away to shoot at. I'm just watching.'

On my third day, I was relieved to receive a radio call asking me to move position. Some comrades on another part of the front thought they had spotted an ISIS fighter. They sent a teenager from the neighbourhood to guide me through the streets to their position. Once there, I installed myself behind a pile of rubble on a slight slope and waited. After an hour and a half I saw a figure moving behind a mechanical digger, freezing for a few seconds, then moving again, then freezing once more. I waited for the next freeze, then fired once, twice, and a third time. There was no more movement.

It seemed unlikely that another jihadi would risk using the same route, so I decided to return to my first position. But as I walked back through the tunnels and curtains, focusing on keeping my shadow from falling anywhere a sniper might see, it dawned on me that I was lost. From the distance I had walked, I should have arrived already. But I didn't recognise anything. I ran across the street. To my left, I could see a curtain and some holes in the walls. I walked towards the curtain. But as I approached it, a voice behind me called out, using our word for 'comrade': '*Heval! Heval!*'

I looked around. There was no one. I continued towards the curtain. *Fzzz! Fzzz!* Bullets hit the ground around my feet. I stopped and looked behind me. *Fzzz!* came another round. Then a hand appeared from a hole in the wall of a house I had just passed, beckoning me. '*Heval*, come back!' came a shout. 'Come back! You are walking towards ISIS!'

Apparently, the curtain I had chosen belonged to the enemy. I ran to the side of the street, leapt through a broken window into what had once been a small shop, kept running, burst through the back door into the street behind, and doubled back so that I was running in the direction of the comrade who had saved me. I arrived a minute later, breathless.

'I saw you,' my fellow fighter said. 'I watched you for a while because I wasn't sure who you were. You didn't stop so I had to fire.'

I tried to push my mistake from my mind. I had walked into ISIS territory alone, which could have been catastrophic. But I hadn't died, and there was no point dwelling on it. When Herdem came to see me again six days later, I was half-expecting Viyan to embarrass me. By sending me to the southern front, Herdem had been testing me. So far I had taken out a single ISIS fighter and nearly got myself killed. But instead of reprimanding me, Viyan declared: 'This guy's a real sniper. He made his base up on the roof and he's been there almost ever since, watching, waiting, day and night, never leaving his post.'

She smiled at me. I tried to look impassive. Herdem considered his reply.

'There is a front in the east that's very hard,' he said. 'The range is very close. It's very intense fighting. It's our most difficult position. But if you want to volunteer, it would be useful.'

With Viyan's assistance, I had passed Herdem's test. Now he was asking me to insert myself into the most important battle we faced.

'Of course,' I nodded. 'Let's go.'

Driving east, the wide-open spaces of southern Kobani were replaced by a maze of concrete canyons, all narrow streets and high buildings. As we approached the front, we had to leave the van and proceed on foot through buildings and tunnels. It was hard going. Many of the houses had collapsed. Every window had been shattered in the force of the onslaught. Chests of drawers, cupboards, satellite dishes, water tanks and railings had been blown into the streets. Peering through cratered buildings and fallen walls, I could see clear through to their back gardens, where plants were dying of thirst and clothes were still flapping on the line. Roofs had fallen in on themselves. Clustered in the craters, I saw jumbles of beds, mattresses, blankets and sheets, brought down from the terraces where the families who had lived there had been seeing out the last of the summer heat. Mixed in with them were glass bowls of tomatoes, grinders and glass jars. Evidently, ISIS attacked on a day when the mothers of Kobani had been making tomato paste.

As we neared the front, the sounds of gunshots, mortars and RPGs became ever louder. I tried to clear my mind. Here the war would be all-consuming. We wouldn't be taking territory block by block. Here we would be fighting room by room.

When we arrived, we asked to meet the two commanders on the eastern front: Haqi, who was leading the YPG, and Zahra, who was in charge of the YPJ. We found Haqi first, in his base up a set of stairs in a ruined building close to where I was dropped. Haqi was in his mid-forties. Short and skinny, with the tan and wrinkles of the farmer he was, I realised when I saw him that I'd met him years before in our territory in the mountains. We'd taken a long hike through the snow to reach some camps high up in the hills and at one point I had wondered whether we would make it. At the time Haqi had been painfully thin, convalescing from a wound sustained in an air strike. Haqi often had a pained expression which strangers mistook for frustration and melancholy but which, after watching him tackle the snow, I understood as what happened when unbreakable will confronts a cold, hard life. I could see he was fitter than before and I congratulated him on how well he looked. Haqi nodded. Then, since Herdem would be leaving, he gave me someone to show me around.

The comrade could not have been more different from Haqi. He looked broken and brought to mind a saying I once heard

81

in the mountains: that if you lose hope, you may find it again, but if your hope dies, all is lost. I followed the man through the corridors, ducking through holes in walls and behind giant curtains stitched together and strung across the streets, up to five stories high. All of them were peppered with hundreds of bullet holes. As the wind blew, it inflated these giant canvases and whistled through their battle scars.

My guide led me to Zahra, who I found making tea in a ruined kitchen. As we introduced ourselves, I watched Zahra place some tissue in a small pot of oil and light it as a candle. Then she took a piece of hard cheese, softened it in water that she warmed over the flame and laid some of it on the seat of a chair. I could see Zahra was not hungry. Still, she wanted to be a good host and make me comfortable, and to encourage me to eat she took small pieces of the cheese as we sipped our tea.

Zahra had been on the eastern front so long that the building in which she based herself was known simply as the 'Zahra building'. It had four floors and stood on the western edge of a roundabout that connected two main roads, one running directly west to east, the other running northeast to southwest. On either side of her building were rows of houses. This was our frontline. In every second or third house we had a unit of five comrades, each of them with their own code name. This meant there were gaps in our line – we didn't have enough people to fill every building – so one of my jobs would be to stop the jihadis sneaking between our positions.

Zahra showed me the garden in front of her building in which the comrades had built two sandbagged bases, one converted from an old garage, the other sheltered behind a wall in which our fighters had dug firing holes. 'They've tried three or four times to take over my building,' said Zahra. I peered over the wall. The bodies of three ISIS fighters lay just on the other side. There were four more out in the street. One man next to the wall had died with his mouth locked open. 'Still trying to catch his breath,' said Zahra.

We mounted the staircase. On each floor I could see the city through large holes made by RPG strikes on the building. On the top floor, the fourth, a base had been fashioned out of oil drums filled with mud and stones. From there, about two hundred metres away across the roundabout and slightly to the south, I had a clear view of a long two-storey building with a flat roof and open ground in front of it. This was Kobani's old cultural centre and it was ISIS' main command post.

Every battle we fought in the city, there would be a building that would become the focus of our nightmares. The cultural centre was such a place. If we could take it over, we calculated we would control a quarter of Kobani. Huge, solid, with a white-and-yellow face, and providing good cover against mortars and heavy weapons, even from a distance I could see the centre would make an ideal sniper base, commanding a view of the entire street below, and an observation point from which to monitor the ISIS-controlled houses in the street opposite and another running perpendicular to it. From the roof, Zahra pointed out the enemy positions on either side of the building. Their main one was the centre itself, said Zahra. 'There's constant movement there,' she said. 'Last night, our sniper killed two of them. You're going to have your work cut out for you.'

My best position was on the roof of Zahra's building. But because the top floor was taking steady fire, I decided I would shoot from the third floor, which had better cover. Due to all the RPG holes in the walls, it was far from safe. Still, I had an idea for protecting myself that I had been wanting to try for a while.

I took a ball of wool that I had been saving, wound it around a sharp edge in an RPG blast hole that looked directly out at the ISIS positions and, keeping it tight, stretched it to the back of the room. I marked the spot on the wall, then, taking a hammer, went around behind it and knocked a hole in it about a foot wide. The two holes lined up with a view of the cultural centre and a long straight street running out to the eastern outskirts of the city. When I looked through them, however, I could see that I was still slightly exposed. So I repeated the procedure, stretching the wool from the second hole to a third wall behind me, marking the spot once more and making another hole so that all three were in line. Beyond that back wall was the building's stairwell. I grabbed a table and jammed it into the bannisters, steadying it with some pillowcases that I filled with earth. I put another pillowcase of mud on the table and, after testing it with my weight, laid my Dragunov down on it and checked the view. I could see clear through all three holes to the cultural centre and the giant red-and-blue curtain the jihadis had erected. From their point of view, however, it would be almost impossible to see me, let alone for an opposing sniper to line up his shot to pass through all my holes.

I wrapped myself in a blanket and lay down behind my Dragunov. The main street down which I was looking, to the side of the cultural centre, was about thirty metres across. The range of my targets started at about one hundred and fifty metres and extended to two kilometres in the far distance. I could also see several hundred metres down three other streets stretching away to the east and the south. I spent three hours observing. There was no movement. My attention kept being drawn back to the large screen made out of red-and-blue curtains that ISIS had hung from the left side of the building to block our view of the street, which was billowing in the wind. I could see that what I had taken to be one giant piece of fabric was in fact two separate parts held together with clothes pegs. Both parts had been strung on a white wire stretching from the side of one building to a lamp-post. The wire gave me a thought. I hadn't fired a Dragunov since Jazaa. I wanted to hear its sound again. I also told myself I needed to check my new base. We were short of ammunition. But I could try just one bullet, just to see how it felt.

I told the comrades in my building that I was going to shoot. The curtain was about one hundred and fifty metres away. I dropped my crosshairs on the cable and, when I was ready, I began breathing out.

One . . .

Two . . .

Keeping my aim, I began squeezing the trigger. Punch. The curtain dropped and hung limply across the street.

'Yeah!' shouted the guys with me. 'You really did it!'

One comrade ran downstairs with excitement. I could hear him below, shouting about what had happened. There was a rush of other comrades up the stairs to my position. They looked at me, and at my holes, and the curtain. Zahra came. 'You brought the curtain down with a bullet!' she grinned.

I was a little embarrassed. It was a lucky shot. But the others kept telling me that I was being modest, and word spread. Weeks later, Nasrin told me how, all the way over on the southern front, she'd heard about how I'd shot down a curtain from three hundred metres. People would ask her to do the same. Comrades even started trying to do it themselves. A few days later I came across a fighter in another building with a BKC who was blasting away at the enemy. I took a hole next to him and waited for ISIS to appear. I could see nothing.

'Where are they?' I whispered.

'Who?' he shouted above the noise of his weapon.

'ISIS!' I hissed.

'I'm trying to bring down the curtain!' he yelled.

All through the war I'd be introduced as the sniper who shot down curtains. The truth was that I might have fired a hundred times and never hit that wire. But on that one occasion, the curtain came down and ISIS couldn't use the street any more – and that was undeniably in our favour.

After a few days, Haqi came to fetch me. He took me northeast along our line, showing me a building where there had been a lot of movement. Opposite was a new four-storey block of apartments under our control. It had been built to house several generations of one family. Most of it was empty, set aside for children and grandchildren who might one day move in. But the second floor, where the owners lived, was expensively decorated: Persian carpets, hand-carved doors and silk furnishings in the two large bedrooms, ceramic floor tiles and yellow-and-white marble surfaces in the kitchen.

Ascending to the roof, I found I could see into a street directly in front, across which ISIS had hung six curtains, and four more streets, two on either side, down which I could see more than a kilometre. It was perfect. I took a carved door off its hinges and carried it upstairs. To hold up the back end of the door, I ripped out a pole that was carrying a TV aerial and dug it into opposing walls of the top-floor room. Next, I took a pile of sandbags, filled them and built a five-foot wall on which I placed the other end of the door. To add further support to my platform, I collected silk scarves from a chest of drawers in one of the bedrooms and tied them to each corner of the door, and then to the wall. I found a ladder up which I could climb onto my platform. Then I dug sniper holes the size of a fist, one in the wall in front, two more in the walls to the side, and then, for bullet-proofing, surrounded them with heavy marble slabs that I tore out of the kitchen. Finally, I hoisted a mattress onto the door, plus a pillow for my legs and a sandbag for my rifle. The idea was to be as high up as possible – no one would expect a sniper to be lying two metres above the floor – and for every part of my body to be supported and relaxed. Only my eyes and my finger would need to move. Since I was still sniping by day, the entire base took me two nights to build.

Moving between my two positions, I developed a routine. I would wake every morning before sunrise, when the Islamists would pray and change shifts. That was always a good opportunity to spot them. The early morning sun also assisted me. Even if they were hiding behind curtains, in the morning their bodies would throw long shadows that peeked out from underneath as they ran back and forth. I almost never managed to hit the first figure I saw. I shot a number of the second or third figures, however, six from my position in Zahra's building and four or five from my second nest. After several days of this, a few of the jihadis started running across my line of sight carrying metal doors on their backs as shields.

The quiet times were the hardest. We knew the enemy was there. But if you couldn't see him, it preyed on your mind. Zahra, though, never seemed affected. She was constantly visiting the front, checking in on each of us, and giving us her broad smile. Later, I discovered she had been raised in a refugee camp in Iraq after her parents had fled Turkey. To watch her was to understand that the hardship in her life had shaped the character she had become. A lot of the comrades were like that. You rarely met one who needed lessons in resilience. More likely, even amid the devastation, was a kind of incongruous cheerfulness. If I was on duty through the night, as the sun was coming up I would say into the radio '*Rojbas*', which means 'Good morning', and from all over sentries would respond with a chorus – '*Rojbas!*', '*Rojbas!*', '*Rojbas!*' – as if we were neighbours in some quiet and orderly town greeting each other on our way to work.

By now we were regularly coordinating our advances with warplanes from the US and other countries. When I had arrived in September, the US were flying only a few bombing sorties a week against ISIS. But by October, in response to our dire situation, Secretary of State John Kerry had convinced more than sixty countries to join the US in a coalition to intervene against ISIS. Our new friends included Britain, France and, at least publicly, Russia and Turkey. It felt like our struggle was finally being noticed.

General Tolin coordinated our attacks with the pilots. She had also decided that when we advanced, our whole eastern front would move forward together so that no unit would find itself exposed. Her strategy was, first, to direct the warplanes to destroy the houses that were one or two blocks ahead of us to create a no-man's-land. In the meantime, our teams would resupply and re-equip, and Zahra and Haqi would plan which unit would take which building. Each ground advance was generally set for the middle of the night. Our fighters moved quickly and secretly, using the shadows. They taped up their ammunition belts to stop them clanking. They even put socks over the outsides of their shoes so that their steps made no noise.

At the moment of an advance, a message would come over the radio: 'Be prepared for the first step.' That meant be ready in five minutes. Then the command would come: 'Now!'

Our tactic was for our men and women to approach a building stealthily, then feel around the door and windows with their fingers for wires and booby-traps. If the door was locked or felt heavy, like it had been rigged, they were to push it open with a broom handle, crouching next to it. If nothing happened, they would enter. If jihadis were suspected to be inside, they would throw grenades through the windows, then enter while opening fire.

Inside these buildings, the dangers increased. One time, I entered one long after our fighters had passed through. After doing my own check of the rooms, I went through to the back door. I was about to step out of the house when I noticed something in the yard that made me freeze: a fishing line and a reel. I squatted down and tried to adjust my eyes to the dark. The fishing line was strung right to left across the yard. Following the lines to the walls, I could see they were hung with mines. Working quickly but carefully, I reached into my pack for some scissors, then began cutting the lines one by one. I must have cut seven of them by the time I reached the back wall. For weeks afterwards I had nightmares about fishing trips with friends going violently wrong.

NINE

Kobani,

October 2014

As the light began to dim in the afternoon of a cloudless, freezing autumn day in late October 2014, word came that we would be attempting to capture the cultural centre. I took up position under a blanket on top of the Zahra building, giving cover. Below me our forces would move forward silently in small units. The plan was for a softening air strike by the coalition to begin at dusk and last several hours. Then different teams would advance to within a few metres of ISIS-occupied buildings around the cultural centre and, once in place, all attack together. After we had captured every surrounding building, our forces would concentrate on the centre itself. It would be bloody, dangerous, room-by-room work and would likely take hours or even days. The only way we would succeed, we told ourselves, was if we observed machine-like discipline.

I watched our teams set off, one hundred and fifty men and women walking without sound, hugging the walls and shadows. After a few hundred metres, they were gone, vanishing into gaps in the walls and the darkness between the houses.

But we had one comrade, an energetic man in his late

twenties from Kirkuk called Guevara, after the famous revolutionary, who had his own plan. From the moment the advance began, Guevara could barely contain himself, sprinting towards the ISIS positions. Soon he started shooting and throwing grenades. As the others tried to calm him, then chase after him, they realised he was moving too fast, skipping past rooms without clearing them, then whole houses. He quickly made it to the walls of the cultural centre. But instead of stopping there, he ran straight past in a wild gallop, right into the Islamist line of fire. By now, everybody was yelling at him to stop. But he kept going. Within minutes he was four or five blocks ahead, out on his own and across the ISIS frontline, with the jihadis between us and him. We could hear him yelling on the radio. He'd almost lost his voice.

Zahra called him.

'Guevara?' she said.

'Yes?' he replied, his voice suddenly soft.

'Can you come back?' asked Zahra.

'Sure,' replied Guevara.

And with that Guevara turned around and started running back towards our lines, hollering and shooting once more as he passed several houses full of jihadis. Our fighters ran towards him, trying to give him cover. As they did so, seven ISIS men ran into the street, shooting at Guevara and at the teams bearing down on them. Within seconds, all seven jihadis were cut down.

And that was it. Somehow Guevara's suicidal run had coaxed all the Islamists into the open. They were all dead. A battle for which we had been preparing for weeks and which we had expected to last all night was over in minutes. The cultural centre was ours. Our fighters ran to its roof, tore down the black and white ISIS flag and hung the Kurdish yellow, red and green banner in its place, and decorated each corner of the building with small YPG and YPJ standards.

A favourite ISIS tactic was to retreat, lull us into a false sense of victory, then counter-attack. As we tried to digest Guevara's extraordinary luck, we steeled ourselves for what we knew had to come. Our guns had fallen silent at around 3.30 a.m. At about four I walked to the cultural centre with Zahra and two novice snipers whom I was training.

As Zahra went to see about erecting more curtains to cover our new positions, the three of us continued towards the centre along a muddy path and through a number of buildings. We passed through a department store strewn with clothes, some of them brand new. I made a mental note to return so that I might replace some of the torn and filthy rags I was wearing. After a few minutes, we found ourselves approaching a small copse of tall pine trees that stood next to the gates of the centre. The gates themselves had been rent off their hinges by a blast of some kind. Through a shattered window, I saw a theatre: rows of red velvet seats covered in dust and the remains of a sound and lighting rig that had crashed down from the ceiling.

We found our way into a ground-floor corridor. It was blocked by piles of broken statues, traditional Kurdish clothes, bright silks and embroidered white cotton, and even a pair of ancient millstones. It seemed the jihadis had taken offence at an exhibition of Kurdish culture and, with characteristic articulacy, smashed it to pieces. In the hall where the display had once stood I found the walls graffitied with the usual black Arabic lettering: *La ilaha illallah, Muhammadur Rasulullah,* meaning 'There is no God but God; Mohammed is the messenger of God'. To one side, next to a sniper's hole, was more interesting writing, six pin-men symbols next to a name in Russian and a number, giving the range. These were shorthand notes for all the targets available from this one hole, made so that any sniper could position himself here and fire immediately. The use of Russian seemed to indicate snipers from the North Caucasus, probably Chechens.

My plan was to ascend to the roof and prepare a sniper's base inside a small apartment that I had spotted from Zahra's building. The only access was via a central staircase, now exposed to the street after losing all its windows. As we were mounting the stairs, one of my comrades whispered, 'Azad, Azad! Who are they?'

I looked out into the street. Two ISIS fighters, instantly recognisable by their long beards and ankle-length *thawb*s, were ambling across the street below. Maybe they hadn't heard about the battle. Maybe they thought we were busy making our defences. I was close to reaching the roof and could have opened fire instantly. But my trainees below me would have likely been caught in the return of fire.

'Shhh,' I whispered back. 'We're too exposed. Stay calm and keep climbing.'

We hurried to the roof. Below us, one of the ISIS fighters was still strolling down the street, oblivious to our presence.

'Safeties off,' I whispered. 'Let these ones pass. There'll be more. We need to be in position and be sure of our shots so we can get them all.'

As we made ready, I turned to the man who had first spotted the ISIS fighters. 'Take out the next fighter who appears,' I said. Seeing him tense, I tried to reassure him. 'Stay calm. Prepare your rifle. This is the work.'

I fixed my scope at two hundred metres and breathed slowly and steadily. A third ISIS fighter entered the street below.

Suddenly I heard a shot. Peering into the street, I strained to locate the body. But I couldn't see it. I turned to the shooter next to me.

'What happened?' I asked.

He dropped his head in shame. He had pulled the trigger by accident. Almost immediately, we started receiving fire. I told the two men with me that now we needed to make ourselves more secure and, as the jihadis' rounds whined overhead, we crawled away from the parapet on our bellies.

The rooftop apartment consisted of one large room, a kitchen, a toilet, a bathroom and two offices. Small windows in the kitchen and toilet looked out over the front of the building into enemy territory. It was ideal for double-hole shooting.

One of my apprentices started hacking away at a wall separating one office from the kitchen. The other attacked the wall between the bathroom and toilet. The walls were load-bearing, made of thick concrete, and my two comrades were soon exhausted, ready to give up. But the position was too good. I took one of the hammers and started pounding on the office wall. Forty minutes later I went into the kitchen and began on the other side. After an hour, we had one hole. A further hour after that, my trainees had made two more in two different walls, giving us a sixty-degree field of vision. Finally, I dragged over a filing cabinet, positioned it beneath one of the holes and tossed a mattress on top.

We were finishing our preparations when an announcement came over the radio that the Islamists had left a car packed with explosives in front of the building, ready to detonate. Our fighters had fired two RPGs at the vehicle in an attempt to blow the charges but the car had not exploded. Now our commanders requested a coalition air strike: one on the car, and another on a house close by where ISIS had taken up new positions. The radio announcer said the planes were ten minutes out.

We gathered up our equipment and began descending to the ground floor as the countdown came over the radio.

'Five minutes . . .

'Two minutes . . .

'One minute . . .'

By now we were safely behind cover on the ground.

'Thirty seconds . . .

'Ten seconds . . .

'Five seconds . . .'

A couple of seconds later a jet screamed directly overhead. We tensed for the explosion.

None came. I later discovered that at the last second the pilot had been called away to a different target. At the time, all we knew was that we would have to detonate the car bomb ourselves.

We quickly re-entered the building and began climbing back up to the roof. On the second floor, however, one of the YPG volunteers called to me urgently.

'Azad! Azad!' he said. 'ISIS are in that house right across the street!'

'You have a gun, don't you?' I said. 'What are you waiting for? Shoot them! Kill them!'

But the man was terrified. Pushing past him, I dropped to my knees in front of a window and tried to peer into the house he was indicating. I caught a glimpse of two jihadis with Kalashnikovs bolting down the street below me, about a hundred metres away. They were heading for the booby-trapped car, most likely to detonate it. The man in front was in his late forties with long hair, a full beard and black robes. The figure behind was smaller, had no beard and was wearing a red leather jacket.

The second one is too young, I told myself. *He's just a teenager.*

The pair made a dash from left to right across an alley-way, making for a doorway. Twice I fired, and twice I missed. Panicked by my shots, the two fighters changed direction and sprinted away from me. I looked through my scope. The teen-ager was following the older man.

I won't kill a teenager, I told myself. *He could have a life.*

But I had to kill the older man, and quickly. In seconds, the pair would dive into a side street and this man would be gone, free to detonate the car. But it was impossible to get a clear shot. Through the scope, the teenager's head was bob-bing directly in front of the bigger man. I knew what I had to do. I could feel my mind start to collapse with the weight of it.

It has to be now, I told myself. *Any longer and they'll be gone.*

I shot the teenager cleanly in the back of the head. He hit a wall and collapsed on the pavement. The older man turned and ran back to pick him up. I waited for him to reach the boy, then fired as he knelt over him, catching him in the arm and spinning him round. The man dropped the boy and fell to one side. I felt I had him. But in a flash, he was on his feet again, hurling himself towards a nearby door. *If it doesn't open*, I thought, *I've got him.* I fired, the door gave way, and the man vanished.

The teenager's body lay out on the street. I studied him through the scope. His head was slumped between his legs. His red leather jacket was marked by dust where he had smashed into the wall. An image of the older man brushing the boy down leapt into my mind. Maybe he was the boy's father. Maybe his uncle. He would want to take away the body to be mourned and kissed one last time by those who had raised and cared for

97

him. Or maybe the boy was a kidnapped Yazidi, forced to fight his own people. Either way, the boy had to have been the man's responsibility. He would want to come back for him. I'd wait until he did.

'How do you feel about this kill?'

I glanced to my side. Standing next to me was a journalist from our media department with a camera and a microphone. I had heard his question clearly enough. But I could make no sense of it. For close to a year I had tried to shackle my emotions. How did I feel? About killing? About shooting a boy?

'Now is not the time,' I snapped, staring down my scope. 'The enemy is still in the house in front.'

'What is wrong with you people?' the journalist retorted. 'You just shot a jihadi but you're scared of a camera?'

This was insane. 'Go away,' I spat. 'Leave. Me. Alone.'

Ignoring the journalist, I focused on my scope. Ten minutes later, the older man reappeared, sprinting back towards the booby-trapped car. I aimed at his chest but missed and he was gone once more. By now I had been kneeling on the tiled floor for twenty minutes. My weapons, ammunition and grenades were weighing me down and my knees were shaking. I felt someone shove a blanket under them to ease the pain.

Suddenly, I saw movement again. I was about to fire when I realised that I was looking at a car tyre. The older man was trying to distract me. I held my fire. I could sense my enemy waiting, too. Was he trying to get me to reveal my position? My shoulder was beginning to tremble from the weight of my straps. I tried to stay focused. Finally, I dropped the rifle and reached for the straps. The instant I did so, two ISIS fighters ran across the street. It was uncanny, almost as if they had been watching me. Furious, I filled my magazine with more bullets, rearranged the blanket under my knees and tried to calm myself.

After a while I saw something move at the corner of the street. At first I couldn't make out what it was. Then I glimpsed the head of a rocket. The older man had returned with an RPG. All at once, he shouldered the weapon, stepped out from the corner and, as he took aim, looked straight at me.

'RPG!' I yelled to my comrades. 'Everybody down! Take cover!'

I still had him in my sights. I was about to shoot when he ducked back behind a wall. I could see the tip of the rocket protruding. I aimed at that and was about to fire when abruptly the man strode out into the street a second time, the launcher on his shoulder. He was walking directly towards me. Surprised by his boldness, I struggled to follow him in my sights. The man stopped. Through my scope I could see he was looking straight at me.

I fired.

His shoulder dropped. I was sure I'd got him. I steadied my aim for a second shot. But when I looked through the scope, I glimpsed the flash of a rocket flying towards me.

I have no visual memory of the impact. But my muscles still remember being barrelled across the room as though I had been caught by a wave. When I came to, there was dust everywhere. I looked around. One of my comrades was sprawled on the floor, silent and motionless. Another was holding his right arm and screaming silently, two fingers missing from his right hand. A third was clutching his left foot. All his toes had been blown off. I realised I couldn't feel my right leg. I looked down. Blood was oozing from my thigh. I punched it to see if it would respond. Nothing.

Seeing volunteers in the stairwell, I called out to them to help the wounded. Too frightened to enter the room, they hesitated. 'Take the injured out now!' I shouted.

They ran in with blankets on which to carry away the fallen. Seeing one of my trainees among them, I shouted, 'Bring me my rifle!'

The man remained still.

'Bring me my rifle!' I screamed.

Still he did not move. I realised that he was shouting back at me. His mouth was moving but I couldn't hear him.

Someone brought me my Dragunov. I checked the scope – still intact. Dragging my wounded right leg behind me, I crawled back to the window and resumed my position. The waiting began again. Rocket or no rocket, I was going to put a bullet through that bearded bastard's head.

A second blast wave hurled me back against the wall. This time when I came round there was brick and glass everywhere. I guessed the car bomb had finally gone up: it seemed to have been a much bigger explosion. I could feel my strength ebbing. Dragging myself up, I grabbed a Kalashnikov from the floor and hobbled to the stairs. ISIS would be sure to attack in force any minute.

Once on the ground floor, I limped through the front door of the building and sat down in the road, legs splayed, not bothering with cover. As I waited for the blast cloud to subside, I lined up the Kalashnikov's sights on where the bearded man had been hiding. I was sure he would attack from out of the dust. *I'm ready for you*, I thought. *I'll destroy you. I'll eat you alive.* This jihadi had wounded my friends and me. He was not going to survive the day.

Behind me, I heard a voice calling me: 'Azad!'

I turned around to see Zahra. My hearing was returning.

'Azad, come,' she said.

I shook my head. 'I'm fine,' I said. 'I'm OK.'

Zahra called again, more of a command this time. When I refused a second time, she turned to a group of YPJ beside her and said, 'Bring him in.'

The women approached. Something about their quiet and insistent manner persuaded me to let them lift me under my arms and drag me back inside the building. Reinforcements were arriving and began shooting towards the ISIS positions. 'My name is Nuda,' puffed one of the women carrying me. 'Give me your rifle and put your arm around my shoulder. I'm taking you out the back.'

Nuda walked me out to a backyard where a pickup had arrived to take away the wounded. I radioed in to say I was returning from the frontline, then climbed into the cab.

A few houses back, I was carried into a basement where our fighters had set up a medical centre. We didn't have a qualified doctor, only a fighter who had seen wounds treated before. He cut away my trousers with a pair of scissors. Sweating and blood-spattered, he asked whether I wanted anaesthetic.

'I can't feel a thing,' I replied. 'Just do what you need to do.'

He gave me a shot anyway, then started digging around in my wound, trying to locate the shrapnel. I realised that my fellow fighters were in the basement too. The man I'd thought was dead turned out to have been only knocked unconscious. The other two, bandages wrapped around their missing fingers and toes, hobbled over to ask how I was. I told them our 'doctor' was having a hard time finding the shrapnel.

The medic regarded me. 'Why are you smiling?' he asked.

'You want me to cry?' I replied.

'I can't find it,' he complained.

I pointed to another hole on the other side of my leg.
'Maybe it came out the other side,' I said.
At that point, I think I passed out.

TEN

Mahabad,

2002

In 2002, when I was nineteen, I was accepted to attend university. But my grades were insufficient for a scholarship and, too proud to ask my father for a loan, I declined the offer of a place. In Iran, my decision had profound consequences. Two years' military service was compulsory for every man in Iran. As a graduate, I would have been able to join as an officer. But as a school-leaver, I would be conscripted as a foot soldier.

I detested the thought of joining the army of my occupiers. But the way Iran's bureaucracy worked, even if I went underground as a full-time activist, without my certificate of military service I would never legally be able to work or own a business or become a husband or a father. I considered joining the Kurdish freedom fighters. But Shina, who had visited the camps, said Komala's armed wing was inactive and uninspiring. Also, I didn't want to leave my family. In the end, I decided that I had little choice.

I walked to the police station in Sardasht and handed over my identity documents to the military registrar. A few months later, my mother received a phone call summoning me to the

103

bus station. When I arrived, there was a minibus waiting and a small queue of young men. We were told we were going for three months' training in Mahabad, a city two hours away.

We were taken to a military barracks outside Mahabad. Once we had passed through the large metal gates and were inside the ditches and barbed wire, we were shown to a building that looked like a factory, which contained hundreds of bunk beds in three rows. We were stripped of our clothes, given a buzz cut and handed a uniform and a tiny grey blanket. Then it was lights out. At half past five the next morning, we were woken by an officer shouting that we had three minutes to be up and dressed. Thus began my short, ignominious career in the Iranian army.

The training, conducted under the slogan 'changing donkeys into men', was mostly an exercise in tedium, centred around learning by rote. We were instructed in Shia Islam, the glories of the Iranian revolution and Iran's great victories in the Iran–Iraq war. We were taught elementary soldiering and tactics. We were shown how to use and maintain weapons: mortars, rifles, Kalashnikovs and heavy machine guns.

Mainly we learned to endure injustice. The barracks ran on the principle of collective punishment. If anyone was late, or untidy, or caught smoking, or talked at night, or stood out of line, or even fell out of bed simply because he was unaccustomed to sleeping in a triple bunk, his whole unit had to do squats or stand outside in the cold, sometimes until dawn. Recruits who answered back or fought the trainers were thrown into solitary or prison. Worst of all was when the officers added days, weeks, sometimes months to your two years of service.

The oppression, bullying, insults and humiliation were relentless. To my mind, they were also pointless. This was no way to build fearless soldiers or create brotherhood. This was how to ensure disloyalty, disunity and meekness. The only part I enjoyed was hiking in the mountains. Recruits who fell behind were forced to carry stones in their packs. But I just ran and ran. If I put enough distance between me and the drill sergeants, I found it was possible, just for a moment, to imagine I was free.

When my three months' training was finished, I was posted to the city of Urmia on Iran's western border near Iraq and Turkey. There was something strange about the unit to which I was deployed. Everyone in the ranks seemed to be Kurdish and from Sardasht. The officer in charge, Colonel Abbasali, was Iranian but the word was that he had been chief of internal intelligence in Sardasht for eight years.

In Turkey, a brutalist state simply denied that Kurds or Kurdistan existed. In Iran, the authorities were subtler. They used the word 'Kurdistan' freely, even adopting it for the name of a small northwestern province. The most senior administrators would take pains to flatter us, hailing Kurds as the most ancient of peoples whose antiquity was sanctified in the Koran. 'We are brothers,' they would say. 'And you are the eldest in the family.'

But it was all lies. Iran's religious police shot dissidents. The regime had no intention of allowing their declarations of equal stature to translate to equal rights. Advantaging Persians and excluding Kurds – and Azeris, Baluchis, Ahwazis, Lurs, Mazandaranis, Gilakis and many others – was how they divided and ruled those they oppressed. Their public praising of us was a calculation. They were daring us to call their bluff, treating us as outsiders and third-class citizens and all the while telling us we were superior to them. Their way of making it difficult to hate them was telling us they loved us.

It says something about human vanity that such tactics were

often effective. But in our people's defence, the Iranian state was a very skilled deceiver. Col. Abbasali, for one, carried off the act faultlessly. He was warm and charming, with an approachable humility that belied his position. I watched him methodically make friends with everyone in our unit. Many apparently believed that he was genuinely their ally and confidant. A number openly admired him and tried to emulate him. Others cooperated not out of innocence but a cynical desire for position and money. Those, like me, who refused to be complicit in our own oppression were a minority. And an unliked one. We had to avoid loose talk. We kept to ourselves.

I did find a friend in Urmia in whom I could confide, however. Qader was older than the rest of us, a career soldier in his mid-thirties who was happy to take the state's rials but had managed to hold on to his soul. When Col. Abbasali told us that we didn't have to wear our uniforms when we went on operations along the border and that our traditional Kurdish clothes would suffice, Qader told us not to listen. Abbasali was only pretending to be giving us the freedom to dress how we liked, said Qader. What the colonel had neglected to mention was that the infiltrators for whom we would be searching were Kurds like us. 'The colonel is hoping your dress will confuse them,' said Qader. 'They're trying to manufacture a situation in which Kurds kill Kurds.'

I wanted to know more. When I questioned Qader further, he told me the 'enemy' we were expected to fight were the PKK, or the Kurdistan Workers Party. Iranian state propaganda described them as traitors. Back then, I knew nothing of the PKK's ideology. But I knew they were Kurds fighting for Kurdistan, and I wasn't about to go to war with my own people.

A few weeks after I arrived in Urmia, I discovered a village near our camp had a *hammam*, a hot spring bath, and I was granted permission to walk there and take a wash. Once in the village, I found a public phone to call home and speak to my father. When I had been conscripted, one of my main concerns was that at some point I might have to take a life. Now I had learned that I would likely be shooting at fellow Kurds. When my father answered, I told him I wanted to desert. He advised against it.

A few days later, it was Eid and I was given leave to travel back to Sardasht. When I walked through the door, I told my parents, 'I'm not going back.'

My father didn't challenge me. The decision was mine alone, he said, and whatever I decided, my family would support me. Then he gathered the entire family and all our neighbours for a huge dinner where everybody was so kind and thoughtful in the ways they entreated me to return to the army that I felt I couldn't refuse. That was something I always loved about my father. His friends beat their sons into submission. My father used persuasion. We might have lived under the yoke of the state, but inside our family my father was teaching his children how to discuss and debate as free people.

Once I was back with my unit, we began going out on patrol through villages near the Iraqi and Turkish borders. We kept it up for four months, hiking, tracking and camping out in the mountains for four or five days at a time. One day, high up above the snowline, we walked through the fog all day until, without warning, we came across a PKK camp in a wood. The guerrillas had just left. I could see piles of cigarette butts where the lookouts had stood watch. The fire was still burning and there were potatoes and onions frying in a pan. 'Careful,' warned Qader as I eyed the food. 'It might be booby-trapped.'

A few weeks later, we were out in the mountains again, way up in the snow near the border. Col. Abbasali was taking us to a peak from where we would be able to look down on a PKK position. After climbing all day, we reached the summit around 4 p.m. But as the lead man approached the top, he was immediately fired on. *Fzzz! Fzzz!* The bullets were passing close over our heads. We threw ourselves to the ground and inched forward on our elbows.

From the lip of the ridge, I could see a deep valley below us, with several mountain ranges behind. Far away below, three men as small as ants were shooting up at us and taking cover behind several big boulders. *Fzzz! Fzzz!* Their bullets were getting closer.

'Bring me the BKC,' said Col. Abbasali. 'Bring me more weapons.' He grabbed a Kalashnikov and started shooting. 'Be clear what you're firing at,' he ordered. 'Shoot to kill.'

It was an idiotic order. There was little chance of hitting a target at that range with a Kalashnikov. Seeing my expression, Qader told me not to worry. 'Just pretend by firing over their heads,' he said.

After fifteen minutes of this, Abbasali's voice came over the radio, ordering me to reposition myself on a small hill in front and fire down into the valley. I moved as instructed. But at that altitude even breathing was exhausting, and when I reached the new summit I lay down in a small ravine and, without meaning to, fell asleep. I woke up to find the radio operator nudging me with his foot and holding out a handset to me. I took it.

'You're sleeping!' shouted Col. Abbasali over the radio. 'I can see you! You've been asleep since you got there!'

He was swearing, revealing his true colours by cursing my family and my people. I was incensed. But his words also removed the last of my doubt. This was my land and my people.

Abbasali was the intruder. He was trying to make us kill each other.

I climbed back up to his position. *If he touches me*, I told myself, *I'm going to shoot him. Then I'll go down to join these Kurdish fighters.* A thick fog was coming in, hiding my expression as I walked towards Abbasali. But when I reached him, he seemed to take the measure of me. He looked in my eyes. He noted the grip I had on my weapon. He did nothing.

Up there on the ridge, being ordered to shoot and kill my countrymen, something crossed over in me. Forced to choose between my people and their persecutors, I made my decision. This was the dilemma that had haunted me since my conscription. Abbasali's pursuit of the PKK meant there was no avoiding it any longer. As long as he kept us out patrolling the mountains, the same thing was going to keep happening. Abbasali was giving me no alternative.

The fog grew thick enough that I couldn't see the end of my arm, and we had to descend. After several hours' walking down the mountain in silence, until long after it was dark, we found a village in which to camp. When it was my turn on guard duty, I relieved my predecessor, waited until he was snoring in his tent, then laid my Kalashnikov on the ground and walked out of the camp into the mist.

I walked through the night, heading down the mountain. Around dawn, I came to a village. I took a minibus leaving for Urmia, then another going to Mahabad, then walked across the city to Shina's house. He was shocked to see me but ushered me inside. I was a deserter, hiding from one of the world's most repressive regimes. But finally I was free.

ELEVEN

Kobani,

November 2014

After capturing the cultural centre, I think all of us had had the same dangerous thought: we might beat them. Alone at night, in the quiet of a turn on watch or during an unguarded daydream, the idea grew in us that the ISIS tide was ebbing. The evidence was there with every forward step we took.

Nobody spoke about it. Saying it out loud would bring it into the world and such a fragile and premature idea would never survive in such a place. We had reached this point by focusing only on enduring and surviving – and only by enduring and surviving would we continue. On our backs we carried our homeland and the friends we had lost. Lifting up our heads to survey our progress, even for a second, was how we would get them blown off. Death was everywhere. Even if we did rout ISIS and take back our land one day, hundreds more of us would die before then. Besides, we had only recaptured a few hundred metres of devastated streets and a handful of smashed buildings. Swapping one set of ruins for another hardly guaranteed the liberation of this small town, let alone Rojava, and we could lose what we had won in seconds. So we buried our hope deep in our broken land, like pirates hiding secret treasure, praying that we might return to find it some day in the future.

I put my effort into returning to the fight. My medic had confined me to a logistics and supplies base a few hundred metres behind the frontlines. When Herdem came to see me, I told him the injury to my leg wasn't crippling and that I should get back to the front.

'To reach the front, you need to be able to walk,' Herdem observed.

'I'm going whether you send me or not,' I replied. 'Besides, the doctor told me that I need to exercise my leg.'

Without taking his eyes off me, Herdem radioed the medic. The medic told him that, yes, I did need to exercise my leg, but no, he didn't consider the frontline the best place for recuperation.

'I'm not going to be running around,' I protested. 'I'm just going to be lying on a mattress behind a wall.'

Herdem smiled. The next day, he accompanied me as I hobbled through the streets to our new front. We found Zahra, who invited me on a tour of our positions. I wanted to see Nuda to thank her for dragging me back from the front. But it took me all day to limp around our new lines and it was not until the evening that I came across her on the second floor of a ruined house, the last building on our eastern front. She was wrapped in a blanket, her eyes red, her face drawn and her hair matted with dust. Recognising me, she got up slowly and we joined a group making tea. We sat there for a while in silence, looking at each other and drinking from our glasses. I felt something pass between us, a warmth between two human beings in a shattered house on the edge of a cold and bitter war.

*

The next morning, almost without thinking, I found myself up before sunrise, climbing inside a ruined building a block from the cultural centre. From my new position, I guessed we now held a little more than a third of the city. I tried to tell a group of comrades setting up in a building across the street where I was so they wouldn't shoot me or leave me behind. But I was in pain, they were exhausted, and neither of us had the strength for talking. When they didn't hear me, I just turned around and worked my way up to the roof.

My new building was a wreck: parts of the balcony and the walls had collapsed, and much of the floor had fallen through. I didn't have the energy to build a nest right away. Instead, I grabbed a blanket I found lying in the rubble, threw it over the debris, lay on it, then pulled a couple of empty sandbags over myself, much as Yildiz had once suggested. The blanket was very thick, with a beautiful design – scarlet and olive and sea-blue in a finely knotted pattern – and I had picked a good spot: from where I was, I could see the entire front and a large building known as the Black School, which was ISIS' new base of operations.

But lying out in the open under a cloth covering, I was exposed – to the wind, the cold and the eyes of my enemy. As the sun rose, I realised the light would reveal my position to any ISIS sniper just as clearly as I could now see their new lines. The pain in my leg was also wearing. Around 10 a.m., I decided that, whether or not anyone had me in their sights, I had to move. When I tried, however, I realised I couldn't. My leg, previously frozen in a spasm of pain, was now numb. I couldn't feel anything below my waist.

I was debating my next move when the mortars started up. I

113

saw the first round arc through the sky, then land a few blocks ahead of me. The second came a block closer. The gunners were sighting their weapons. Shells were rolling steadily towards me like a wave. As one round hit, another would already be flying behind it through the sky. Watching one, I caught a flash of blue. I'd heard the jihadis had worked out a way to attach a detonator to the nose of a gas canister and fit fins and a tail to its base. This had to be the result. The gas bombs were said to be capable of bringing down entire buildings. If one hit my roof, I was done for. But if I moved I was finished too. ISIS marksmen would be watching the bombardment to cut down anyone who ran. I comforted myself with the idea that a flying gas cylinder was not a precision weapon. If I was equally likely to find myself underneath a gas bomb wherever I went, then it made just as much sense to stay put as to move elsewhere.

A mortar landed a street away. Another landed in the building opposite. I hugged the floor. Out of the top of my eye I saw a dark object nosedive in front of me, disappearing into the floor below. The building bounced. I saw another mortar overhead. A building to my left leapt in the air, then collapsed. Another mortar flashed just over my head. I was in the air. I was on the ground. My eyes and nose were stuffed with dust. I scrabbled sideways, into the stairwell. The mortars kept coming.

I might have lain in the stairwell for a minute or an hour. When the barrage began to ease, I hit my legs and rubbed them to bring them back to life. I checked myself. No blood.

In front of me was a small, unfurnished room, the doors blown in but three walls still intact. As I stirred, the noise seemed to alert someone on the other side of the wall. Through a broken window I saw a pair of eyes looking back at me. I thought I recognised them.

'Who are you?' the man demanded in Kurdish. He seemed alarmed.

What was his name? Where had my voice gone?

'Who are you?' he shouted again.

I wanted to reassure him, to call him by his name and tell him it was me, Azad. He would know me if I could remember his name. But already he had his gun up. It was probably too late.

'Azad!' I managed. 'It's Azad!' I held up my hands. 'Comrade – it's me, Azad. How are you?'

Slowly, the man's eyes and face opened. He dropped his gun and walked on.

As I watched him go, his name finally came to me. 'Qandil!' I shouted after him. 'You're Qandil from South Kurdistan!'

He kept walking.

After the mortar attack, I didn't object when Zahra suggested I spend my nights back at the cultural centre, our new logistics centre, now five hundred metres back from our new front. I was there on a foggy, freezing, rainy evening a few days later when an explosion tore through the air and the radio began screaming: 'We are under attack! We are under attack!' Another voice shouted: 'We need bread, now! We need bread!' 'Bread' was our code for assistance.

Instinctively I grabbed my rifle and limped to the roof to provide cover. It was pouring with rain. Rounds were *fzzz*ing past. Up ahead it looked like New Year: sparks were flying through the air in every direction. I could hear gunfire and the jihadis' cries of '*Allahu Akbar!*' Every few minutes there was a deafening explosion which seemed to lift up the houses and walk them towards us. The sharp tang of explosive hung in the air. On the radio, I could hear a commander calling his teams but getting no response. Others were shouting. 'We're being attacked on our left flank!' 'We need more ammunition!' 'We need assistance now! ISIS is coming around the side!'

After a few minutes, I saw Yildiz run past on the street below, M16 in hand. I was no use where I was, so I hopped down to the street after her. The wounded were already starting to arrive, their blood mixing in with the mud. Some were screaming. Others, missing a leg or holding their guts in their arms, were past that. More and more kept arriving, until we had twenty men and women lying down in the street, rolling in the mire, crying out in pain. I tried to help one man, a big comrade, who was crying out and bleeding from the stomach and the leg. But as I put my hands under him, a shock of pain ran through my body from my wounds and I felt myself fainting and collapsing backwards onto the street.

'What are you doing, Azad?' a comrade yelled at me.

I was doing nothing to help. I could only watch. I pushed myself against a wall, trying to melt into it, and observed as my friends and comrades were brought in dying. Others ran around trying to save them. When I couldn't hear or see any more, I covered my ears and closed my eyes and let the rain wash away my tears.

Walking the scene the next day with Yildiz and skirting what remained of eight ISIS suicide bombers, I listened as she described the battle. ISIS had mounted an intense counter-attack using waves of kamikazes. It started when one jihadi drove a car into our lines and detonated a pile of explosives. That was the cue for a second car bomber to race in and detonate. A third then did the same.

The three explosions knocked out the two teams either side of them, breaching our line. ISIS then sent in ten suicide bombers on foot through the gap. They ran through our lines and headed for the most crowded area they could find. 'They had dressed themselves like ninjas, all in black, with only their eyes showing,' said Yildiz. 'They didn't blow themselves up straight away. Only when they failed to break through our lines or were stopped, that's when they exploded.'

Yildiz had brought two of them down herself. 'Through my thermal, I saw this guy looking around a corner of a house,' she said. 'He was trying to find a way forward. I fired. He exploded like a balloon. There were pieces of him everywhere, all over the walls, and a pile of mincemeat where he had been standing.' Of the second bomber, she told me, 'I shot him in the head through his moustache. He was wearing a vest of explosives and he had his finger through the pin of a grenade in his vest.'

I went to look. The man's forefinger was still hooked through the grenade pin, frozen in place. His face was like a stopped clock.

Thirteen of our men and women died instantly in the attack. Twenty-three more were wounded, seven of whom died later. I knew three of those killed. Qandil was beheaded and dismembered by the blast from one of the car bombs. Nuda had been defending her position in the building where we had shared tea when a suicide bomber ran into the ground floor, detonated his device and brought the building down on top of them both. Guevara also finally ran out of luck. He had become separated from his unit and, though they told him to wait, he ran to them anyway. Rounding a corner at his usual sprint, he found himself confronting two of the bombers. They shot him in the arm but he kept running, firing as he did so and yelling on the radio to his comrades: 'I'm fine. I'm doing well. I'm coming to you.'

TWELVE

Kobani,

November 2014

Every day brought another storm. We were united in trying to save our city. But so many of us were being cut down it was difficult to know whether we were fighting or dying together.

One day in early November 2014, as I crossed the street, I ran into Hayri as he emerged from the ruins of a building. He had grown a short beard but he still looked neat and tidy, with the same scarf around his neck. He had been stationed on the front next to mine for a month, a kilometre away, but in all that time I hadn't seen him. Now he was being redeployed. We looked at each other. Hayri had one hand around his Dragunov and his trigger hand in his pocket. He smiled.

'Everything good with you, Hayri?' I asked.

He nodded. 'Yes, it's good, it's good,' he said. 'We are good. And you?'

I told him I was fine.

Hayri was jiggling something metallic in his pocket. He showed me: a clutch of M16 bullets. He said he had found them in a house that he'd helped capture. 'They were on the floor in a bedroom,' he said. He wasn't sure if they had been left behind by dead comrades or by jihadis he had killed.

'Use them,' I said. 'You'll need them.'

'You sure you don't need them?' he asked me.

We chatted for a little while longer. Then he walked on.

I recall almost every word of that conversation. Every time I met someone, I tried to fix them in my mind and my heart in case I never saw them again. It might not even be a bullet that would take them. My wound, though still raw and bloody, was closing up. But by now all of us were living on the cusp of exhaustion. After two months with only scraps to eat, our flesh lay like sheets over our bones and our eyes were sinking back into their sockets. Tiredness ate at our minds and confused our bodies. One evening, curled up in the base, I woke with a start, my heart bursting. I was sure I had been shot. After checking myself all over and finding nothing, I realised what I was feeling was not a fresh injury but the muscle memory of being caught in an RPG shockwave. This went on for months.

To keep my focus, I tried to eliminate everything from my life but the craft. Planning, watching, firing; cleaning, building, hiding; deceiving, breathing, withstanding – this became my character. A rifle is a machine with an unswerving function, fast and powerful, speaking only when it must. To be right with the rifle, to be its friend and comrade, I had to be the same: just being and acting. I went for days with my mind blank and my mouth shut. It wasn't that I had nothing to say. It was that I had found a different way to say it.

But everybody has their limits. Once, after a long day watching the street, I saw a jihadi walking towards me. There was something disgusting about this man. Under his headdress he had yellow teeth and eyes, his mouth seemed to be in the middle of his face, and he was covered in filth. He was acting crazily, just strolling in front of his curtain in the middle of the road. Just at the moment when I had his head in my crosshairs, he turned to look at me. I was about to fire when suddenly I heard the word '*Rojbas*'.

I looked up to see a comrade looking down at me.

'Why did you disturb me?' I demanded. 'Why didn't you let me kill him?'

He looked around the empty room. 'Who?' he said.

I sat up. I was under a blanket in a corner of a room. My rifle was leaning up against the wall beside me.

I was far from the only one corroded by fatigue and hunger. I began to observe a new phenomenon among a few of my comrades. When we were waiting for the next battle, every-one would be vigilant, kept awake for days by the terror in our imaginations. But the moment a fight started, the instant we could see the shape of the next attack and even that there was a possibility of living through it, some would relax and fall asleep, right there in the middle of a firefight. One time I watched a group of our fighters take it in turns to spray the inside of a room in a building they had just taken over, only to discover that inside it was one of our own, asleep. The man dozed on even after his comrades shot a book-case down on top of him. We were moving forward, of that there was no more doubt. But it was an open question how many of us were even capable of reaching the finish.

In mid-November the Islamists introduced a new tactic that seemed to speak of an impatience with our resistance. I was making new holes for a sniper's nest high up on the top floor of a wrecked building one afternoon, trying to work out how to be safe behind a wall that had a giant five-metre crack in it, when suddenly the gaps in the wall on either side of me exploded with ricochets. All along the front I could hear what sounded like a huge firecracker, a rolling *crack-crack-crack* that lasted several seconds.

Almost immediately, voices began screaming for assistance on the radio. When I went to investigate, I found every base had been hit. There were pools of blood on the floor in every position we held. Comrades were pushing past me, ferrying out the wounded and the dead. What had happened?

We concluded that ISIS' commanders had instructed every one of their men to fire all their guns at once. They had unleashed a deadly volley along the entire front. Ten of our men and women perished in the fusillade. Another thirty were injured. With so many bullets fired at the same time, some found unlikely trajectories. One of our team commanders was shot and killed when a round that had already travelled several hundred metres passed through a hole in a wall and then a tiny gap between two sandbags. It hit him right in the forehead.

Most of us viewed ISIS' new strategy as another obstacle with which we had to cope. But Herdem saw it as something we could turn to our advantage. Why not use ISIS' tactic against them? he asked. Why not make it even more deadly, so that we fired into their gun holes not just along one front but across the whole city? Four days later we did just that, firing every weapon we possessed at a prearranged signal on the radio. I emptied several magazines. It was devastating. We killed scores of jihadis and wounded many more. You could hear them screaming and panicking all along the line. A few days later we did it again, then again, then again. I don't know why the jihadis never repeated the tactic against us. But we were happy to steal it from them.

*

Day by day, week by week, we inched forward. In late November, Herdem's voice came on the radio, asking me where I was. I told him I was in a tall building close to an old girls' school which at that time marked the beginning of no-man's-land. An hour later, Herdem found me. With him was a new comrade with a boyish face, blue eyes and ginger hair whom he introduced as Servan. Herdem took me aside. 'He's very polite, a very good person, very honest and quiet,' he said. 'He can also hit targets extremely well. But he has no sense of tactics and doesn't understand bases or keeping himself safe. I need you to teach him.'

I was doubtful. Servan seemed to have the calmness and patience of a good sniper. But I could see just from looking at him that he had no feel for the psychological side – the ability to calculate, analyse and manipulate. Despite my misgivings, I found myself warming to him. After more than two months of shooting and deceiving and lying in the dirt, there was something refreshing about Servan's pure nature. You felt you had no choice but to protect such innocence.

The next morning, when I woke at half past four, Servan was already up and waiting. We walked together to the front, leaning into an incline and a wild wind that was rushing through the streets. Our new target was the Black School, which stood on a hill with a wide view over the city and which had earned its name from the black mesh barricades nailed across its windows. It was another building of huge strategic value. If we captured it, we would control more than half the city.

Once we arrived at the front, I told Servan to stay put in a tall four-storey building under the control of a women's team commanded by a YPJ leader called Sama. I was going to check along the front for firing positions that would allow us to target the Black School and another nearby college in ISIS hands. I was ascending the staircase of a building next to the college when I heard several dozen ISIS fighters shout their war cry: '*Allahu Akbar! Allahu Akbar!*' The chorus came from around two hundred and fifty metres away and was followed by the noise of an arsenal of guns firing. The Islamists were making a fresh attack.

I ran to the roof and hurried towards the parapet. Abruptly, ISIS stopped firing. That was the signal for around twenty jihadis to appear in the street three or four blocks away, yelling and running towards our lines. Another ten were running across the rooftops.

I lay down and fixed my scope to two hundred and fifty metres. The jihadis filled my sights. I started shooting into them, once, then again, then a third time. Two or three collapsed while they ran, to be trampled by the others. A dozen or so reached the college and started sprinting across the playground. They were heading for one of our teams but, out in the open, had no cover. I continued to fire at them as they went. Another down. And another.

They were running over each other now.

I took down another.

And another.

I switched to the figures on the roof. I took one more. Then a second. A third to the side.

I switched back to the playground. The jihadis were scattering for cover behind a small wall and shouting at each other to fetch their fallen comrades. Then they began running back towards their lines. I hit one of the bigger ones in his side as he ran away from me. He pirouetted around and dropped to the ground. A friend grabbed him under his shoulders and tried to drag him off. I hit him too. By now several of my comrades were also firing, including one on a BKC and another on a mini

Dushka. A few more Islamists fell. Then they were gone and the attack was over.

I was ecstatic. I had shot twelve jihadis in two minutes. What an opportunity! The right place. The precise time. Even if I was wounded, I could still be part of it. I was still effective.

After a while, I remembered that Servan wasn't with me. I descended the building and went to find Sama. She told me Servan was above her on the top floor. I climbed up. On the higher floors of this building almost the entire facade had been obliterated. What remained was punctured by holes the size of basketballs. Instinctively, I threw myself to the ground and tried to find cover. Servan, I noticed, was lying directly behind one of the holes, his rifle protruding into the street.

'Servan!' I shouted. 'You can't lie there! Move away! Get out of there!'

Servan got up and ambled over to me.

'What are you doing?' I asked.

'Making a base,' he said. I saw that he had piled up four mattresses behind the hole he had chosen.

'That's not a base,' I told him. 'That's a target. You're right behind a hole. Even someone with a pistol could hit you there. If any ISIS spots you, you're done.'

Now Servan looked worried. 'How do I make a real base?' he asked.

I spent the next hour instructing Servan. I showed him how to stuff the holes with pillows so that his position was concealed. Even then, I told him, he was not to stand behind any hole. I showed him how to build a platform out of shelves and pillows. I told him to set it a few metres back from a small hole and right at the top of the wall, just below the ceiling. 'They're unlikely to shoot the holes at the top as they can't imagine how anyone could be lying down just below the ceiling,' I explained.

Servan was excited by what he was learning. 'Great!' he kept saying. 'Great!' Once I was sure he knew what to do, I went downstairs to talk to Sama. When I came back up, to my amazement Servan had nearly finished his base. 'I used to be a builder in Aleppo,' he grinned. Once he was done, Servan built me a base too, on the other side of the building.

We stayed in our building for three days. Nothing was moving. On the third afternoon I heard a noise that sent an electric shock through my stomach. Scanning the horizon, I saw a familiar outline in the distance, crossing the street from one side to the other, billowing black smoke and crushing debris beneath it. I froze. It was the first time I had seen a tank in Kobani. What could rifle rounds do against that?

I grabbed my radio and asked for Haqi. When he came on, I blurted out, 'There's a tank, between the Black School and the college! It could obliterate us all!' I requested he talk to the coalition about an immediate air strike.

From its position on the hill next to the Black School, the tank would be able to fire down on a large section of our front. I made a quick calculation. There was no doubt the tank could blast Servan and I out of our vantage point high up in our buildings. But because its barrel couldn't dip below the horizontal, it would have more difficulty hitting the fighters below us.

'Everybody down to the ground now!' I shouted.

I stayed on the top floor. Sama arrived with an RPG and a bag of rockets. 'The air strike won't make it in time,' she said. She ran to the roof.

I could hear the tank moving again. I thought I could see a plume of black smoke behind the Black School. To the side of

126

Top Herdem in Kobani. The picture is part of a series by AFP photographer Bulent Kilic that have become iconic. Herdem was killed a few weeks later. (BULENT KILIC/AFP/Getty Images)

Above left Hayri in Kobani. This photograph captures Hayri as I knew him: surrounded by destruction but somehow cheerful and pleased to see you. (YPG archives)

Above right General Medya (right) with Evindar, a team commander who died in the battle to take back Sarrin. A veteran of more than a decade of fighting and a capable and intelligent warrior, Medya was the perfect soldier to face ISIS. (YPJ archives)

Above Yazidis entering our territory after fleeing ISIS's attempted genocide on Mount Shengal in Iraq. Our volunteers stalled the ISIS slaughter, allowing 500,000 to escape. (Emrah Yorulmaz/Anadolu Agency/Getty Images)

Left Zahra. Raised in a refugee camp, the hardship in Zahra's past seemed to have given her an indomitable spirit. Here she is pictured on the roof of the Zahra building. (YPJ archives)

Left My view of the cultural centre from the Zahra building. (YPJ archives)

Above The battle for Kobani. This picture was taken from the Turkish side of the border in October 2014. (Emin Menguarslan/Anadolu Agency/Getty Images)

Below Around 70 per cent of Kobani was flattened during the battle to save it from ISIS. This picture, taken in January 2015, shows the extent of the damage. (BULENT KILIC/AFP/Getty Images)

Abdullah Öcalan, our leader. For two decades he has been locked away on a one-man prison island off Istanbul. (YPG archives)

Guevara. One of most enthusiastic volunteers, his suicidal charge into and beyond the ISIS lines won us the battle for the cultural centre. (YPG archives)

Above left Nuda. When I was wounded, she and other women carried me out of the line of fire. She died a few weeks later in an ISIS suicide attack. (YPJ archives)

Above right Servan. One of our most gifted marksmen, Servan's innocent nature meant he never learned the deception and manipulation that a sniper must also deploy. (YPG archives)

An air strike on Kobani in January 2015, in the last few days before we took the city. (Associated Press)

Above Herdem with Keith Broomfield. Keith had made some bad decisions in his life, so his journey to becoming a freedom fighter was a shining example of human redemption. (YPG archives)

Left Tolhildan (left) with his brother. Three brothers from the same family joined the YPG, which was a strict violation of the rules. Tolhildan refused his mother's entreaties to leave Kobani. (YPG archives)

Herdem with the nine jihadis he killed single-handedly. (BULENT KILIC/AFP/Getty Images)

Gunter Helsten had served in the German army and French foreign legion. At 55, he was a father figure to many of us. (YPG archives)

The graveyard at Kobani. (YPG archives)

A field of spectacular red fritillary flowers at the foot of the Zagros mountains. To us, the red fritillary denotes the death of an unknown warrior. (YPG archives)

the building was an abandoned, rusty yellow combine harvester. From behind the harvester came more noise and another jet of black smoke, then the tank's nose rumbled into view. Its barrel swung around until it seemed to be pointed directly at me.

Fire spat from the barrel. The shell flew towards us and crashed into the floor below. The building shook like the branch of a tree. When the dust cleared, I caught sight of the tank backing up and disappearing again. But after a few seconds I heard it advancing once more. As soon as it appeared, it fired again, this time directly towards Sama. The shell went wide. Through a crack in the floor above me, I saw Sama drop to her knee with the RPG over her shoulder. She fired.

Her grenade missed by inches and slammed into the harvester. Sama, shrouded in dust, immediately reloaded and fired again. Then again. Then one more time. All her shots slammed into the harvester. By this time I had run up to the roof and was racing across to her.

'Wait!' I shouted. 'You're hitting the harvester! The tank is to the left.'

We waited for the dust to clear. But the tank had gone. A fighter jet screamed overhead. Half an hour later, a predator drone began circling. We never saw the tank again. But for the rest of our time in Kobani, we all felt its presence around the corner.

Come late November, ahead of our planned advance on the Black School, coalition planes had been hitting ISIS' lines for days, raining down five-hundred-pound bombs guided by our spotters on the ground. Watching the planes from below, we could feel the world coalescing behind us. A month later, after

127

two Islamists massacred twelve journalists and staff members at the offices of the *Charlie Hebdo* magazine in Paris, we watched as a French female pilot screamed overhead all night, bombing ISIS in run after run. She radioed our air coordinator on the ground. 'I am a member of the YPJ too,' she declared.

The air strikes were devastating. One rocket could blow a hole the size of a swimming pool in a building. The detonations would send eruptions of dust and debris hundreds of metres into the sky. Even if the jihadis survived, many would be deaf, blind and numb. Even so, this remained a street war. ISIS not only held its ground, often the jihadis counter-attacked during the strikes, trying to mingle with our forces so the strikes would stop. You had to respect their courage. Hundreds of them were vaporised but they were not giving up.

Once we reckoned the jihadis had been pummelled enough from the air, our teams would advance on foot. At this stage, the strikes would become as much a risk to us. Crossing no-man's-land on the southern front one day, five of our men and women were killed by an errant bomb. There was also no way of knowing where ISIS had set mines or hidden pockets of fighters. And now that the jihadis were in retreat, sniping was becoming one of their favoured tactics. Rather than give cover from the rear, I began to advance with commanders directing the attacks. As he or she went forward, I tried to shoot down any Islamists fleeing the bombardment or staying behind in no-man's-land. There were always a few die-hards.

The Black School attack was no different. We set off up the hill on a dark night in late November. As we were advancing, a coalition bomb wounded three of our fighters. To my left, one of our snipers cut down three jihadis holding out in the front yard of the Black School. After suffering a few more casualties and killing some more jihadis, we took the building. I'm sure I

128

took my share of shots and kills, but now I struggle to remember how many. For weeks it had been just steady, methodical slaughter. When I try to recall that time, what I remember most is a vague feeling of rhythmic accomplishment.

THIRTEEN

Iran to Europe,

2003–2004

When I look back further, to the days after I deserted the Iranian army, when I was still just a teenager taking on God, Iran and any other injustice or untruth that offended me, I can't help but smile. Such stubbornness. So alone. In those days I had no way of knowing the turmoil my actions would unleash. But even if I had, I don't think I would have hesitated. What connects the child I was then to the man I am today is purpose and spirit. Back then, I was just a boy who liked to go swimming in a mountain stream. Today I am a freedom fighter, a veteran of fifteen years of struggle. But I am not changed. That's who I was then. It's who I am now. The path between these two figures is bounded by turbulence. But the way is straight and true.

I probably should have left Iran the day I deserted. I could have simply walked over the mountains to the PKK's camps. But it was never my wish to abandon my family and friends. Shina and I also wanted to stay and fight for our rights.

We lived together as subversives for more than a year, sleeping during the day and leafleting at night. Many other young men had deserted and were doing the same work. The numbers didn't make it any less dangerous. Dissidents like us were jailed or 'disappeared' in their hundreds.

Perhaps inevitably, one day Shina returned to the house with news that his name was on a watch-list. It couldn't be long before mine was too. A few days later we heard that the authorities had raided a garage owned by my father where I'd been secretly storing books and newspapers. A day after that, while we were out, security officers broke into the house where Shina and I were living, searched it and questioned the neighbours. Shina and I had to disappear immediately.

Shina decided that his colleagues in his movement, Komala, could hide him. That night, after so many years as friends, we said farewell. It would be an age and thousands of miles before I saw him again. Unlike Shina, I wasn't ready to put my life in the hands of others. My only choice was to leave Iran immediately. At first, I had no idea how I would do this. Given the unpopularity of the regime, however, perhaps I shouldn't have been surprised to walk into Mahabad's market and find a people smuggler sitting in an office just off the main square.

Mustafa was an older Iraqi man from the south of his country with a crippled leg and a walking stick. He specialised in trafficking what sanctions had made attractive to middle-class Iranians: colour televisions, laptops, rare teas, French crystal, candlesticks and Chinese porcelain. Mustafa had the air of a wealthy man, well groomed and at ease. His office, however, was stark and bare. Mustafa, I guessed, hid his contraband outside the city.

Mustafa spoke plainly. He could send me to Europe. Passport and identity papers were no problem: I wouldn't be going through any checkpoints. I said I needed to be sure of the route and that there was no risk of being captured either by the Iraqis or the Turks, as either one would probably send me back to Iran. Mustafa reassured me. Though I would have to pass through at least one of those countries, he said, I would not be stopping.

Where did I want to end up? asked Mustafa.

Europe, I replied.

Mustafa nodded. The price was seven thousand five hundred dollars, he said. We shook hands.

The only problem with my plan was that I didn't have a rial to my name. But others were willing to help. In 1997, when Saddam once again turned on Iraq's Kurds, this time massacring a hundred thousand, tens of thousands had fled across the border into Iran. We had distant relatives in Iraq – my father's aunt had married a Kurd on the other side of the border – and when the refugees began arriving, my father went to the frontier to see if our relatives were among them. He waited for hours. Towards the end of the day, he noticed a man with his wife and their three girls, standing in the rain, cold and hungry. 'They looked like the branches of a willow tree,' my father said later. 'Slack and listless, dragging themselves along the ground.' My father approached the man and said that since all Kurds were family, the man was welcome to bring his wife and children to stay in our home.

The five of them were with us for a few months before they were accepted by the UN as refugees and given a new home in Canada. While they were living with us we discovered the man had a heart condition that required pills, and since the medicine was cheap in Iran, my father bought him an enormous supply. From Canada, the man wrote to say he had found a job as a gardener, bought a house and was sending his girls to a Canadian school. He called my father 'brother' and my mother 'sister'. Now, when he heard I was in trouble, he wrote to say he would gladly lend me the first payment of three thousand five hundred dollars. He did not know how the money would be spent. He just knew that I needed help.

This was wired to Mustafa. I told Mustafa I would borrow the rest from my extended family. We agreed a system of payment by stages. The money would be held by an intermediary, a doctor and mutual friend whom everybody trusted, and released bit by bit according to how far I had travelled. Mustafa told me he was satisfied with the arrangement. I was to make ready to leave in a few days. There was no time to say goodbye to my family.

A day later, I took a bus from Mahabad back to Urmia, close to the border with Turkey. I had nothing on me apart from some chocolate, a water bottle, five hundred dollars and my family's phone number in my head. In Urmia, a man was waiting in a pickup to take me to the border. In a clearing off the main road, a group of seven weathered-looking men were saddling twenty horses ready to depart, directed by another man in a filthy overcoat who appeared to be in charge. Most of the animals were carrying barrels of diesel and petrol. Several of us who were travelling to Europe would be going at the same time. The plan was to head out that evening, cross the border high up in the mountains during the night and be inside Turkey by the following morning. The smugglers gave us tea and yoghurt to fortify us. Then we set off.

We started climbing immediately. We passed through thick forest, followed narrow paths up precipitous ravines, crossed mountain streams, hugged cliffs and, finally, leaving the trees behind, pushed up into the snow. It was a dark and moonless night, and freezing cold, but my horse was sure-footed and I felt the exhilaration of a new journey underway. I became mesmerised by the way the horse's metal shoes would shoot out sparks when they struck crystal and flint on the path. The smugglers, too, were formidable, walking all the way, never tiring and always making sure the horses were calm and still had spirit for more. 'Why don't you ride?' I asked one. 'Can't afford to,' he puffed back. 'The horses are reserved for cargo.' At times, we could hear Turkish border guards close by and we had to hurry away. 'For the next ten minutes, you just ride as fast as you can,' the head smuggler would say, and off we would go, galloping into the night, racing ever higher into the mountains.

Some time in the night, we came to a clearing by a river. I heard voices. Then somebody shone a torch in my face. 'Stop that!' I shouted angrily. 'You are blinding me!'

The head smuggler came to talk to me. 'These people are PKK,' he said. 'They're collecting donations.'

I refused. I had been forced to leave my home partly because there was no active revolution in Iran for me to join. To my mind, the militants were a disappointment. 'I'm not going to pay,' I sniffed. 'I don't want anything to do with them.' The smuggler shrugged and handed over ten dollars on my behalf.

Finally, we neared the pass. The wind was roaring and piercing. I could feel my horse tiring. The smuggler urged me not to let him stop for anything. 'If the animals stop moving here, we'll never get them going again,' he shouted over the wind. We crested the pass and began descending the other side. A green morning light started to creep up into the sky. After an hour or two we came to a village where the smugglers called a halt and fetched water for the horses, and lentil soup for us. I ate, then fell asleep where I sat, leaning against the wall of a village house.

*

Later that morning, I awoke to the sound of an old taxi struggling up the track into the village. Now it was daylight, I could see there were five of us Kurds travelling to Europe – me, three other young men and an older man with a prosthetic leg – and we crowded into the car, which took us further down the valley to a bigger village, then onto smooth asphalt. The driver gave my travelling companions and me a Turkish identity card each. When he dropped us at a bus station on the edge of a city, these allowed us to buy tickets.

For the next few days we skipped across Turkey from city to city in small journeys of a few hours. Always there would be a smuggler waiting in a café at the next bus terminal who would buy us our new tickets and direct us to the next middleman along the route. Soon we reached Istanbul. What little I saw of the city seemed immense, a wonder of noise and light and strange food smells. But we were quickly ushered through the back streets to a house where we were shut in with dozens of others.

All were hoping to travel to Europe. Many had run out of money and were in limbo, waiting for a relative to send more cash so they could restart their journeys. We were told none of us could leave the house, so we sent somebody out to buy food for us. That evening they called our five names, then took us to a lorry park where we were told to climb into the back of a truck transporting planks of wood. We waited for an hour in the dark, silently eating biscuits and drinking water. Then we heard an engine start and we were en route again.

After seven hours, we stopped at what we took to be a checkpoint. We waited silently and without moving. After a while, we drove onto what felt like a ship. The boat sailed through the night. The next day, the lorry disembarked in what we guessed was Greece. Hours later, it pulled off the main road. The doors were opened. We were in a forest. A man took us to a small, abandoned cottage – ugly, with broken windows and dirty floors – where there were around seventy other people: Afghans, Pakistanis, Iranians, Arabs and Africans. Some had been there for months. A lot of the talk was about the scores of refugees who were said to be drowning in the Mediterranean or suffocating in the back of shipping containers. Refugee graves were now said to dot the route.

On our third day in this ruined house, a smuggler came and asked me to call the doctor to release another payment. I refused. 'I'm hungry,' I said. 'I need food first.' So these rough-looking smugglers, unshaven and covered in badly drawn tattoos, took me out to a restaurant. I ate well. I smoked a few cigarettes. Then I called my father.

'I am OK,' I told him. 'I am here.'

'Who are you?' my father replied sharply. 'Where is my son?'

'Father, it's me, Sora!' I said. 'It is your son!'

'What blanket do you use when you sleep?' demanded my father.

'Father, for God's sake, I can't remember,' I replied.

'Who is your best friend in the neighbourhood?' he insisted.

I said the man's name.

'Describe our house.'

I described it.

My father considered my answers for a moment. Finally, he relented. 'OK, OK,' he said. 'But you sound very strange, my son.'

Reluctantly, my father agreed to call the doctor and ask him to send more money to Mustafa.

*

That conversation with my father was my first experience of how misunderstanding can often be measured in kilometres. It had been more than a year since we had spoken, as it was always my mother who was home whenever I called. I later also discovered that Mustafa had told my father that he could guarantee to take me somewhere but not necessarily that I would arrive alive. My father, it seems, had convinced himself that there was a good chance I was already dead and an impostor was trying to take my place.

A few days later I was taken to another lorry with the four other Kurds. It was a refrigerated trailer, full of chocolate. That lorry just drove and drove. We huddled against the cold in the back as best we could. After what seemed like most of a day, we stopped once more in another hidden place in another forest, and again we were led to a house crammed with people. By now we were losing track of how long we had been travelling like this, in and out of windowless trucks and abandoned houses in nameless forests. But after a few more days, we five were loaded once again into a car, driven into the hills to a lorry park, pushed into a trailer full of baby milk and transported for seven or eight hours. When we stopped, the doors were opened to reveal another lorry park, and a smuggler hustled us across to another truck and trailer that contained a few cardboard boxes. This part of the journey was especially secret, the man said. The driver wouldn't know we were on board. Once we arrived at our destination, said the smuggler, 'we will wait for a few hours and then we will come for you. At that point, our job is done and you'll be on your own.'

We hid quickly behind the cardboard boxes and the smuggler closed the doors. After a while, the driver returned and started his engine. He drove for an hour. Then he slowed for what seemed like a series of checkpoints. The time taken to negotiate these barriers made us suspect that the authorities knew someone was inside. Then the doors opened. Someone called for us to show ourselves. I stayed where I was, hidden under a pile of boxes that I had pulled on top of me. Three of my travelling companions were also well hidden. But the older man had left his prosthetic leg sticking out. They found him and took him away. Then – miracle! – they closed the doors once more. After that, we felt the truck board another ship. It sailed for a few hours, then we disembarked.

We wanted to know where we were. The sides of this truck were made of canvas and one of my companions cut a tiny hole in the fabric with a little knife he had so he could try to read the road signs. But he couldn't understand them. When I looked, I saw a blue sign that read 'London'.

'We are in England,' I announced.

There was a murmur of approval from my three companions. Though I hadn't said where I wanted to go, evidently the others had been more specific. I suggested we bang on the cab so the driver stopped. I was planning to hand myself over to the police. But my companions had arranged to stay with relatives. We were still discussing what to do when the man who had cut the hole in the canvas interrupted us.

'There are two police officers driving alongside us,' he said. 'They're looking right at me.'

'There's no way they can see you through that tiny hole,' I replied. 'You're just scared.'

But after a few minutes, the lorry slowed down, pulled over on the side of the road and parked. Then two police officers opened the trailer doors.

'How many?' asked the officers.

There was no point hiding any more. We had arrived safely, and we were exhausted. I held up four fingers. Behind them, I could see the truck driver was furious. He was shouting and pointing at us. He grabbed a tyre iron and started swinging it, ready to attack. 'If he attacks us, we attack him back,' I instructed the others. They looked terrified.

In the event, a police officer pulled the driver to one side, a police van arrived and we were shown into a little cage in the back. The other men were dismayed at the disruption to their plans. But I was so happy. My only ambition had been to leave Iran. Now, when the police officers closed the doors behind us and took us away, the noise had a finality to it. There was no going back. I was twenty years old, I had made it safely to Europe, and my new life could begin.

FOURTEEN

Kobani,

November–December 2014

As we steadily took back Kobani street by street in the last weeks of 2014, we discovered the jihadis had left us some surprises. The remains of takeaway food, still in its plastic cartons. New cars and motorbikes, often with the keys still in the ignition. The morning after we took the Black School, a comrade discovered a tunnel inside a nearby house, dug straight down into the earth then angled directly towards our lines. They had been trying to dig under us so as to be able to pop out and attack us from behind. Inside was a wheel-barrow to move the earth, a generator to power a drill and a battery-powered lighting system.

The next day I was scouting the area for places where Servan and I might build new nests when a comrade ran in shouting, 'A sniper has been shot!'

I froze. 'Where?' I asked.

'That building over there,' replied the man. He pointed at a neighbouring block, next to a building where I had told Servan to wait.

'Where is Servan?' I asked. 'Has anyone seen Servan?'

There was silence.

'Take me to the sniper,' I said.

Numbly, I followed my comrade into the neighbouring building. It had been nearly levelled by air strikes and we had to climb up a two-storey field of rubble to get inside. The building was like a skeleton: the stones and bricks had been blasted off and only the steel remained. There, on a small piece of floor that was somehow still intact, I found piles of sand drenched in blood. As I squeezed onto a small ledge that had a clear view over the city, I saw Servan's dark-grey baseball cap lying on the ground, blood all over it. The way it was lying suggested it had fallen off his head as his comrades carried him out. There were two fighters crouching on the ledge. Advising me to stay low, one of them told me Servan had taken a shot to the left side of his face, just above the eye. He had probably died instantly. Even if he hadn't, there was no way he could survive losing all that blood.

I shuffled past the two fighters. In a corner with a wide view over the enemy front I found Servan's scarf, backpack and rifle. I could see he had been working on a new hole, just as I had taught him. There was a pair of pliers there, with which he had been bending back a piece of metal that was blocking part of his vision. To get the purchase he needed, he would have had to lean out of the building and expose himself fully to the enemy. I like to imagine the danger didn't even cross his mind.

We were now in control of more than half the town. But we had lost more than a dozen people capturing the Black School, and I had lost Servan, and as the battle for Kobani ground on, our worlds narrowed until it became impossible to imagine a horizon beyond those tunnels and streets or even to think back to yesterday or forward to tomorrow.

I felt angry that I had been asked to care for Servan. I was angry that he had extracted my affection so easily, then abandoned it so carelessly in the dust. I couldn't move on from his death, as I had from so many others. When someone dies in your care, maybe it is right that you are haunted for ever. But there was something else. There had been times in Kobani when I was awed by the depth of human resilience, and others when I marvelled at how conflict sharpened our senses. Now I wondered whether darker forces were at work. Servan had been a flower, so polite, so pure, and his innocence had killed him. He had been too good to live. What did that say about those of us who remained?

Servan's loss made me unsure of how to interact with other people. Was I clear when I spoke? Did I give too little or too much? Where did I get my conviction that I was right? Servan had been sent to me to train. Now he was dead. What if I'd radioed him to sit tight and wait for me to help him make his hole? What if I'd been more explicit and detailed in my instructions? From then on, everything I did took on even greater seriousness. There was no place in my life for much more than mechanical exactness. Servan's death taught me that even one wrong or omitted word might be fatal. I began to see things in purely binary terms: black or white, life or death, friend or enemy. I was far from the only one.

One night I was scanning the streets we had captured around the Black School when I caught a glimpse of a figure about four hundred metres away moving furtively and tensely from shadow to shadow, checking left and right like a thief. At one point, he entered a building and vanished. When I finished my shift the following morning, I went to the logistics centre to ask if we had anyone stationed in the house the man had entered. A group of wounded men lying on the ground shook their heads. A fighter called Janiwar jumped up and suggested five of us go to check.

We found the house and began to search it. After a while, one of them called over to me: 'Azad! Come. We've found something.' I followed him through the kitchen. 'There's someone sleeping there,' said one of my companions, gesturing through a window that looked out onto the garden. I peered through. There was the shape of a body under a blanket.

'Is he one of us?' I asked. 'Do you know him?'

They shook their heads. Janiwar spoke up: 'He has to be ISIS. Let's kill him.'

'Let's take him prisoner,' I said.

'What if he has a suicide vest?'

'Fire a burst over his head,' I said, 'then you run in and grab his arms and pin them to his sides. I'll have his head in my sights the entire time.'

They reluctantly agreed. At my nod, the first man fired and the other two ran in and threw themselves on top of the man. The sleeping figure woke with a start. 'I'm Kurdish!' he cried out. 'I'm Kurdish!'

We dragged him out. He looked shocked, as lifeless as a dead body. When I demanded an explanation, he confessed he had been fighting on a neighbouring front and had lost his nerve. 'I can't do it any more,' he said. 'So many dead. I can't fight any more. I ran. I just thought I'd hide out until the city was liberated.'

Fear is contagious. The man's face was a whirlpool of hopelessness. I didn't want to look at it. 'Nobody is forced to be here,' I said, glancing away. 'If you don't want to be here, you don't have to be.' Then I told the others to take him behind our lines, and left.

144

Once out in the street, however, I could hear shouting. I ran back in. The others were beating him.

'What are you doing?' I shouted. 'Nobody touch him!'

'But he is a coward!' they said.

'Nobody has to fight,' I told them. 'That is our belief. We are all volunteers.'

I understood their anger. They were all from Kobani, and had all been wounded defending their home city. Hundreds of us had sacrificed themselves and this man was saving his skin. Black or white. Friend or enemy.

To distract them, I suggested they search him. Out of his pockets came euros, dollars, Chinese money, Georgian money. He said he had taken it from the bodies of dead jihadis. To me, this sordid thieving was a second reason not to have this man in our ranks. To the others, it was something else to punish him for.

We decided to march him to Zahra and let her decide what should happen. Thankfully, she agreed with me. 'He doesn't have to fight if he doesn't want to,' she said. 'He's free to go. But he shouldn't hide here as we might kill him by accident.'

The others argued, but in the end Zahra's word prevailed. I heard later that the man observed Zahra for a few days, deliberating with himself, before asking if he could stay and become part of her team. Weeks later, Zahra told me he had become a great fighter.

The way we were deteriorating was reflected in how grim the battlefield was becoming. ISIS rarely retreated, and every street we took was filled with their bodies. As we advanced, we began to find the corpses of our own people, too, volunteers who had fallen when ISIS first overran them. One day I entered a house

145

on the frontline where five of our fighters had been based, to find them prone on the floor, their hands tied behind them, their heads neatly balanced on their backs. We began to notice that dogs, cats and even chickens were growing fat on this harvest of cadavers. We had to shoot them, to stop the spread of disease.

The bizarre landscape that Kobani was becoming offered some surreal moments. One team, finding themselves in a sugar store, built a base out of fifty-kilo bags. Every time they were attacked, the bullets would tear into the sacks and cover them in a sweet-tasting cloud. When I visited, I found them reaching into their fortifications for fistfuls of the stuff to put in their tea. Another confusing sight was bits of shop mannequins lying next to real bodies. No clothes store in Kobani, apparently, had been complete without these unblinking pink plastic figures, and months of air strikes had scattered their slender, unbending limbs all over town. When you looked closely, it was clear that many of the mannequins had also been smashed and set on fire by ISIS. It seemed the army of the pure took no chances with temptation, not even with the sexless nakedness of a plastic doll.

Once or twice I even witnessed death take on a kind of winsome quality. Because the Black School was such a natural crow's nest with a commanding view of the city, I based myself there for more than a month. Herdem brought me an M16 with a thermal that we had captured from ISIS. One perishing night in November, around 11 p.m., I was lying on the ice on the roof when, through my thermal, I saw a hole in a wall about a hundred metres away turn white.

Haqi's latest intelligence, gleaned from listening in to a captured radio, was that ISIS would be trying to sneak through our lines and attack us from behind, just as we had done when

I first arrived in Kobani. Haqi had overheard an ISIS commander say they would be coming singly or in pairs.

I was sure this white light I was seeing was the heat signal from a jihadi. I watched it for a while. Was he the commander? Were there more Islamists coming? Did he have night vision? In the end I decided he was a scout, collecting what information he could on our positions from peeking through the hole and listening to the sounds around him. I couldn't let him go.

I fired a single shot.

The heat signal slowly began to dim. I watched the white light fade for a full ten minutes. Then it was gone.

I think we all realised that even if we survived, we would be walking out of Kobani very different people. Our standards for what was normal behaviour had begun to shift. We had one comrade who was always insisting on going forward. 'Why are we taking so long?' he would say. 'Why aren't we moving?' On one occasion some of my comrades had to pull him to the ground when he set out walking alone towards ISIS' lines in broad daylight. When they tried to explain to him that there was a strategy to a military operation, that we had to wait until all our fronts were ready to move forward together, he argued back. The waiting was taking too long, he said. It was costing too many lives. And what were we so afraid of when many of the houses we captured turned out to be empty?

He spoke well and made some good points. But that wasn't it. The man wanted death. After seeing so much suffering and so many lives lost, he wanted to be next. It wasn't that he had lost hope or that he especially wanted to die – and he certainly wasn't about to shoot himself. Rather, he wanted to achieve

147

something, to claim a piece of land with bravery and integrity in the name of freedom, and he had convinced himself that his death was the best way to do it.

I noticed that I, too, had become unafraid of the sound of war. I no longer ducked or flinched at explosions or the slapping of bullets on a wall. I'd even begun to welcome the jihadi cry of '*Allahu Akbar!*' that used to so terrify me. Now it told me where they were. As war transformed me, I understood some changes would be permanent. The lack of sleep, the constant vigilance, the endurance – these things would mark my body and my mind for ever. And while sometimes these alterations horrified me, at other times I embraced them. I might have been surrounded by death but my senses had never been more alive. When I stalked, I was like a leopard, all my senses charged, my alertness so high it was almost deafening. One day when we were clearing a house I burst into a room in which I expected to find ISIS fighters and glimpsed a gunman by the far wall. I raised my rifle to shoot. Then I hesitated. I was looking in a mirror. That stone-faced, cold-eyed figure levelling his weapon at me – that was me. Most people would have been bewildered. I burst out laughing.

All the while as we advanced through Kobani's streets, we felt the presence of fate. When I thought of Servan, I realised that part of me had always thought of him as doomed – that one day, whatever he did or I did, the war would catch him and he would be gone. That was the nature of war: a succession of catastrophes that battered your capacity for endurance, then killed you or broke you or, if you survived, rewarded you with pain or guilt. This was the destiny of all of us the moment we had picked up a gun.

Perhaps hardest to accept was that some of us were fated to die in friendly fire. But a few made their peace with that, too. Chia had been born without a heel on his left foot, or it had been shot off – he never said, and I never asked – and when he arrived in mid-December as part of a group of reinforcements from the mountains, he was immediately given command of a unit on the south side of the Black School, based in a house where the bodies of five jihadis still lay in different rooms.

Because of the danger of infiltration, we had orders not to move around our lines at night and to shoot anyone we saw. I was on watch one night when Sama, the YPJ commander, radioed to say that someone was calling out in Chia's area, likely pretending to be wounded as part of an ISIS trap. I went to check and, as I was passing a house on my left, I heard a noise inside, like someone moving his jacket. Then I heard it a second time. It was the sound of someone getting ready to attack.

I always kept a bullet chambered in my rifle with the safety off – my safety was my finger. As a rule, I also never slung my rifle over my shoulder but carried it in my hands so that I would be ready to fire just by dropping to a knee. That night, for some reason, I had hoisted my rifle onto my shoulder. *I've got no chance to turn around*, I thought. *He already has my head in his sights.*

I walked on as casually as I could towards a deep shadow in the overhang of a tall building on the other side of the street. I passed one house, then a second. As soon as I was safely inside the shadow, I ran for position, spun around and swung my rifle to my shoulder so I had the doorway in my sights. *If I wait for him to show himself*, I thought, *I'll have a chance.*

At that moment, a voice called out in Kurdish from the doorway: 'Who's there?'

I stayed silent.

'Who's there?' came the voice again.

149

'Chia?' I shouted back.

'Azad?'

A figure stepped out of the doorway. Through my thermal I could see him limping.

'I nearly took your head off,' I exclaimed.

Chia walked over to me. 'Azad,' he said. 'I know that when I die, it will be one of us that pulls the trigger.'

It was a strange thing to say, almost like he was forgiving me in advance. But in the end, Chia turned out to be half-right. Months later, I was told one of his own team shot him in the arse during a village firefight. Sent for treatment over the border, the Turks caught him and threw him in prison.

As time went on and our positions became known to the jihadis, we had to make ever more elaborate attempts to deceive them. One day, I was called by a commander named Alisher to his base, a bunker he had built out of cement bags in an old builder's supply store that now formed part of our line. Alisher told me that earlier in the day he had narrowly avoided being shot by a sniper as he walked across his base. He showed me two fresh bullet holes in the wall at chest height. Looking out into the street, I calculated that the sniper must have set up in one of several houses opposite.

I made a plan to make the enemy shooter show himself. By gathering up different mannequin parts from the streets, I was able to piece together a complete figure, which I dressed in a military uniform. Then I asked a new comrade who was an apprentice with me to lie down on his stomach and 'walk' the doll back and forth past the place where Alisher had had his near miss. The doll needed to look as realistic as possible, I said, like someone inspecting the spot where the sniper's rounds had hit.

At about 4.30 a.m., I took up a position on a rooftop one street back, protected by a parapet about half a metre high. The wall was punctuated by several holes, each about the size of a basketball. I lay down behind one that gave me a clear view of the houses opposite and started scanning. The only possible location from which the bullets could have been fired, it seemed to me, was through a small hole in a chimney that was attached to the outside of a building facing me.

I lined the hole up in my sights and waited. It was raining. I tried not to move. But the rain crept into my clothes and slid down my neck like a snake. I felt my body slow. Five a.m. passed, then six. By now it was light, but the winter dawn brought no relief. I was shivering and tensing and willing my body to keep fighting the cold. Seven a.m. By now, I knew, I was losing the ability to do much beyond lie there and wait. Eight a.m. How come I could still feel the cold? I should have lost all feeling by now. Or passed out.

Nine a.m. Suddenly, I saw a small change in the light behind the chimney hole. Narrowing my eye, I relaxed my body, ready to shoot. I wanted my rival to shoot first. When he raised his head to check whether he had hit his target, I would have him.

After a few minutes, I saw another flicker of light behind the hole. Something felt off. Snipers make slow, deliberate movements. The movement of the light had been frantic, like someone waving. Had my enemy somehow spotted the trap I had laid for him? Was he waiting for me to fire so *he* could shoot *me*?

There was another strangely hurried movement of light behind the hole. Quickly, I rolled away, crawled towards the stairs and found a thick wall behind which to catch my breath. How had I been rumbled?

The answer awaited me in Alisher's base. Instead of walking

the mannequin back and forth, my apprentice, perhaps lazy, perhaps scared, had simply propped it up against a wall. The sniper had been able to see that someone was trying to fool him and had reacted accordingly, trying to spring my trap so that he could counter it. I had become the hunted instead of the hunter.

A few nights later I turned on my M16 thermal scope, pointed it towards Alisher's position in the cement store and immediately saw a figure jump over a wall next to it. All week there had been reports of ISIS movements in that location. I fired without hesitation. A gunfight broke out and I ran to the roof to find a better position. When I arrived, I could see several figures on a roof above Alisher's base shooting in. I made a radio call, directing all fire onto the attackers. Then I aimed at one fighter who was firing a BKC directly at Alisher's position and shot.

'Ah, Azad, you shot me!' Alisher cried out on the radio. 'You shot me!'

My whole body went numb. My trigger finger began to shake. I sat up, pushed my rifle away and hugged my knees, trying to breathe. My stomach was tightening into a knot. *What did you do? What did you do?*

After a while Alisher's voice came back on the radio. 'Azad?' he said. 'Azad?'

I grabbed my rifle and ran downstairs. As I stepped inside Alisher's base, I felt the ground move beneath me. I was walking on a body. I felt around my feet. The corpse was warm. It had a long beard. Then I heard a laugh. Alisher was on the other side of the room, watching me. 'I heard you describe my location over the radio,' he said. 'I tried to hide but you were too quick! Don't worry, my friend, don't worry. You only grazed my leg. I don't even need to see a medic!'

Alisher later explained that while I had been running to the roof, ISIS had broken into the back of the house where he had his base. He and his team had had to abandon their position and counter-attack it from the outside. I had missed seeing the changeover and assumed the figures firing in were ISIS. The body I had felt was one of the jihadis that Alisher's team had killed.

Alisher thought my mistake hilarious. I was mortified. It was all I could do to stop my confidence from shattering into a million pieces right there on the ground.

FIFTEEN

Kobani,

December 2014

One afternoon, walking down a street close to the Black School, I caught sight of the outskirts of the city and, beyond it, fields. I was transfixed. My whole world had been reduced to these narrow streets, pushing forward metre by metre. Now I could see that Mistenur Hill was seven hundred metres to my south and, beyond it, open country. We only needed three or four more big pushes and we would have the city.

Suddenly, a firefight erupted around the base of the hill. I watched a big-bellied figure take up a position next to a wall, level a BKC in front of him and fire off almost an entire belt. The man had two other fighters with them. They seemed to be firing down on our forces but at that distance it was impossible to be sure: they might also have been our men and women.

It was unreal just to stand there in the street and watch a battle. Around me, our men and women were strolling un-hurriedly from one place to another, obliviously chatting and laughing. I took cover behind a lamp-post and began sighting my Dragunov. If those distant figures were jihadis, they would be able to see right into the street and shoot our people like

155

chickens. Only one other fighter, Serhad, seemed to under-stand the danger.

'Azad!' he shouted. 'Azad! Shoot them! Shoot them!'

'I'm not sure who they are,' I replied.

Haqi, who was nearby, called around on his radio, trying to get confirmation.

'Off the streets!' I shouted at our fighters around me. 'You're in the line of fire! They can shoot you at any minute!'

It was a mess. Nobody seemed to understand that, though we now held this street, we could still be targets in it.

Haqi called back. A neighbouring commander had told him that, yes, he was being fired on by three ISIS fighters on the slopes of Mistenur Hill.

'Shoot them between the eyes,' Haqi told me.

I lay down on the street. A second sniper, Haroon, took up a position on the roof of a building. As we sighted our weapons, a crowd of fifty gathered. 'The big guy with the BKC is Number One,' I shouted to Haroon above the hubbub. 'The man in the dark green is Two. The one in grey is Three. You go for One. I'll take Two. We'll both go for Three.'

Haroon shouted his assent. The three jihadis were now firing from the corner of a house. We waited for them to reload. Two was saying something to One, who turned around to reply. I counted down to Haroon: 'Three, two, one . . .'

I aimed for Two's chest and neck. Punch. He went down. The crowd cheered. 'You got him!' Serhad exclaimed.

One ran over to Two and tried to drag him to safety. Haroon fired at One. Two was still alive and reaching for his gun. I shot him again. Then I moved to Three. He and One were now sprinting for cover inside a house. Haroon was still firing steadily at One.

'Shoot him!' I shouted.

Haroon fired again. 'He's down!' he shouted back.

Another cheer. The women began ululating. We stayed until nightfall trying to shoot the third man but he never re-appeared. Bored, the crowd drifted away. Eventually, the coalition unleashed a furious series of air strikes on the ISIS positions which were captured on film and broadcast around the world. Mistenur was ours.

The firefight on Mistenur Hill should have been a reminder to us all of an age-old Kurdish truth: even when we possessed territory, we couldn't expect to be safe in it.

That night, scores of comrades came with clothes and blankets they had scavenged and worked until morning sewing together a giant curtain, which they strung from base to base across the road. Despite that, two days later a man from Alisher's team was shot in the head as he crossed the street. When I examined where he had been hit, it seemed that the bullet had to have come from the girls' school that we had captured two weeks earlier. It didn't make sense. Then, a few days later, one of Serhad's team was hit in the leg at a nearby intersection. A day after that another man was shot in the hip as he walked down the side of the Black School. Haqi called me on the radio. I was to stop working nights and hunt down the ISIS sniper. It was clear that ISIS was learning from us and infiltrating our lines to take us down one by one.

I arrived at the scene of the last shooting to find Alisher's team hugging the walls around the spot where the shootings had occurred. 'This is the third person to be killed!' one young woman shouted. She had been with the dead man when he was hit. 'I was just chatting to him and he was shot right in front of me.'

I planted my feet on the bloodstains where he had been shot. Looking towards ISIS' lines, I could see I was protected from every angle by curtains and walls. I sat down against a wall. How was it possible to be hit here? Absently, I looked down the street back into our territory. About nine hundred metres away, I could see a two-storey building jutting out into the road. Windows on its different floors had a good view of the street. After a while, I recognised it as the girls' school. I called Haqi.

'Are we sure that the girls' school has been cleared?' I asked, looking at the building. 'Is the entire building occupied by our forces?'

Haqi said he would check. When he came back, he told me the girls' school consisted of two buildings on either side of the road. We held one part. But the part I could see was in ISIS' hands. This was a grave misunderstanding. We had all assumed we had complete control of the street. In reality, there was an island of jihadis in our midst with a clear line of fire. Right at that moment I was in all likelihood looking down the sights of an ISIS sniper rifle.

Trying not to betray my discovery to the shooter, I walked around the corner as calmly as I could and, as soon as I was clear, started running and turned into a back street that headed towards the girls' school. When I felt I was about four hundred metres away, I climbed up inside a three-storey building that would give me a view down on my target. After crawling into position on a half-collapsed roof, I could see the school playground below me. Moving some bricks out of the way and making myself comfortable, I settled in to watch.

I waited for hours. In the mid-afternoon, I saw two pigeons fly out from a window on the first floor. Someone was walking around inside. I crawled back from my position, took the stairs down a floor and lay upwards on the first few steps of the next flight, looking out through a blown-out wall. From my new position I could see a window on the second floor whose top quarter was open and shielded by blinds. I studied those blinds. After half an hour, I saw a shadow move. I fired quickly, then again, then again, then again. There was a distant return of fire but nothing from the window.

The next day, coalition planes executed several bombing runs on the building. As soon as they had finished, our men and women stormed in and engaged the survivors in a fierce fire-fight. By the evening, the building was ours. Walking through the ruins that night, we found five of our own fighters, killed months before in the ISIS advance. But behind the sniper's window I also found a large, fresh bloodstain and a wide smear running out of the room and down the corridor where his fellow jihadis had dragged the man away.

One comfort we had was that, however worn down we were, the jihadis were just as fatigued. Even their famous suicidal discipline was beginning to crack.

Down one side of the Black School was a street that ran straight and wide, west to east, all the way out of the city. We called it Forty-Eighth Street. Based there was a commander called Tolhildan, one of three brothers who had joined the YPG – something that strictly was a violation of a YPG rule about sending more than one member of a family to the front. When Tolhildan discovered his mother had complained, he called her from his base in Kobani and said, 'Do that again and I'll not call you mother any more. I'll only leave this city dead.' That was a measure of his commitment. So was the way he looked. I was amazed one day when Tolhildan told me he was only twenty-three. He looked forty.

One morning, Tolhildan's voice screamed over the radio: 'They've got a Hummer. We need an RPG.' A machine gunner ran to his position, fired at the vehicle and stopped it. Tolhildan then shot the driver.

Haqi came on the radio. The Hummer, he said, had been on its way *back* to the ISIS lines. It had already burst through our frontline and driven as far as the cultural centre, a kilometre or so behind us, where it had dropped off seven jihadis. They had tried to storm the building, killing three of ours, before scattering. Herdem had brought down two in the street. The surviving five were holed up in a house surrounded by our people. When I arrived, Herdem had already left – 'It's easy now,' he had said – and the others were bombarding them with grenades and RPGs from all sides. All five were dead inside a minute.

Something made me want to see their bodies. Climbing through the house, I found an older one, with blue eyes, perhaps fifty. The others were much younger, maybe seventeen or so, their legs all smashed, their bones sticking out and their faces chewed up by bullets and shrapnel. Later Haqi told me that as they shot at us, the jihadis had been on the radio, asking over and over for assistance. The response? 'God is great!'

One of them had answered, 'I know God is great, but we need help! We need an ambulance! We need another Hummer!'

'God is great!' came the answer again.

'I don't care!' screamed the jihadi over the noise of his gun. 'We need help!'

Three days later, the jihadis drove another Hummer at us. We killed four of the five inside instantly and dropped a grenade on the fifth after he jumped into a well. After that, we brought up a digger to make giant holes in the roads, big enough to stop either Hummers or tanks. We had no doubt we would need them. Retreat seemed to be making the jihadis even keener to throw themselves into our guns.

SIXTEEN

Leeds,

2004–2011

After a few weeks in a refugee centre in Ashford, southeast of London, I was told I had been assigned a place to live while my application for asylum was considered. A minibus picked up a few of us, skirted east London and drove north, dropping off the others at hotels and guesthouses along the way. I watched the English countryside pass by. The farmers were at work in the fields, cutting hay, harvesting wheat and setting fire to the stubble. They had bigger tractors, the grass was more lush and the gardens behind the endless rows of houses seemed too small for growing many vegetables. Otherwise, I was struck by how familiar the scene looked.

After six hours, I was left at a hostel just south of Leeds in a city called Wakefield. There were four floors in the building, with eight rooms on each, plus a shared toilet and a kitchen. My housemates included another Kurd, a few Iranians and two Africans. No one spoke much English. But we were all in the same position and my new housemates were kind, showing me where to buy food on the small allowance we were given and where to find a bus into town.

Once a week, I would call home and speak to my mother, father and sisters. They would always tell me that when they spread a rug on the floor and set it for dinner, 'your place is empty'. I missed them terribly, of course. But their words reminded me that I was on my own, and it was up to me and me alone to make the most of my new country.

The summer of 2004 was a tempestuous few months of storms, floods and blazing afternoons in England – not the fog or placid grey drizzle I had read about in children's books – and I took advantage of the warm spells to explore my new home on foot. Wakefield was an ancient market city, once a centre for wool, cloth, grain, coal and cattle trading, built around a grand yellow-stone cathedral. A cool wind blew in off the Pennines to the west, sweeping past red-brick buildings and the old mills down on the River Calder. It was grander and prettier than Sardasht – some of the main streets were quite beautiful – and everything was spotless. I was astonished by the buses, whose arrival at a stop was announced in advance on an electronic board and timed to the minute. How different from the drivers in Sardasht, who made their passengers wait for hours as they crammed their vehicles ever more tightly.

On my first wander around town, I stopped for a while on a bench near the cathedral. I was curious to see people feeding the pigeons. Back home, we would have shot and eaten them. The way people dressed and walked was also interesting. There seemed little difference between men and women. I even saw one man pushing a pram. When I was a boy, my father used to carry me on his back but he was an exception, and his friends would tease him about it. In Wakefield, men and women seemed content to be equals. Another surprise: contrary to what I'd heard about British reserve, people were friendly. On my first day, I was approached by a young couple who could see

164

that I was lost, or at least new, and who wanted to help me. I didn't need their help but I was touched by their kindness – and so embarrassed by my inability to thank them that I resolved to learn English as a first priority.

At the hostel, I found an English dictionary and started with the 'A's. My primary-school English started to return. Soon, by applying myself for an hour or two, I was able to decipher the letters I was receiving from the Home Office detailing the progress of my asylum claim. After a couple of weeks, I was given my own apartment in a house: a bedroom, sitting room, bathroom, toilet and kitchen. It was more than generous. I wasn't allowed a television – I couldn't afford a licence – so in the evenings I listened to the radio and practised my English.

Under the conditions of my temporary stay, I was allowed to study but not work. I enrolled in English classes at a college of further education in town. I also found an illegal job at a fruit-packing factory on the city outskirts where a lot of refugees worked. I had to take the baskets in which the fruit was trans-ported and lay them on a conveyor belt which passed through a stream of hot water. I hated it. The CCTV cameras and the punch-code entry system made the place feel like a prison. My fellow workers timed their work to the second, dropping what-ever they were doing the moment it was break time or the end of their shift. I quit after three days. But I quickly found more work, as a waiter and cook in a Pakistani restaurant in Leeds, working part-time and weekends.

Slowly, Wakefield and Leeds became my life. I passed my driving test. I saved five hundred pounds, bought a car and became the restaurant's delivery driver, taking curries all over the city. One day I received a letter telling me my asylum appli-cation had been approved. I was given a council flat in Leeds. Transferring my English course to a college in the city, I studied by day and drove by night. In time, I paid back my family's friend in Canada. I developed a taste for fish and chips and full English breakfasts. I went to a nightclub. I had a girlfriend, then another. I spent my weekends travelling up and down the country, visiting Liverpool, Edinburgh, Portsmouth, Southampton and London, touring monuments and old houses, hiking in the soft rain and swimming off the beaches. What I enjoyed most was the freedom to do whatever I wanted. One day at college, I wrote an essay about winter in Sardasht, describing the snow and how people dressed. My teacher, an Australian woman in her sixties, showed it to her husband, a university professor, and he wrote me a note saying he thought I could be a writer one day. I'm sure he was just being polite. But I was delighted by the possibility the professor's words implied: that in Britain it was perfectly reasonable just to wake up one morning and decide to be a writer. This was what it was to be free.

My gratitude towards my new country didn't mean I was uncritical of it. Like many, I was sceptical of the American and British military occupations of Afghanistan and Iraq that followed 9/11, which seemed to be less about defending freedom than pushing smaller, weaker countries around. But I remained just as distrustful of religious hardliners. A handful of the mosques in Leeds were regressive, dictatorial and explicitly exclusive. Their imams would tell their congregations that they were living in a land of unbelievers. They said that Islam required them not to interact with British people. I found this attitude hypocritical and dangerous. These people would enjoy the security, rights, prosperity and welfare the unbelievers gave them, while secretly encouraging their flock to despise them. A year after I arrived, four British Islamists, three of them from Leeds or nearby, killed fifty-two people in simultaneous bomb attacks in London. What struck me was that, although the bombers had never even been to the Middle East, in their pre-attack videos they cited the Saracens and the Koran as inspiration. It reminded me of how the authorities in Iran had used the same things to sow fear there.

As the novelty of my new life began to wane, I also found myself slipping into the immigrant's paradox. To Westerners who have never emigrated, the idea that a person might pay thousands of dollars he didn't have and risk his life travelling halfway around the world only to arrive in a new place and surround himself with people from his old life can seem a contradiction. Actually, it is much the same instinct that sees Britons fly around the world on holiday, only to herd themselves into replica 'pubs' serving pints and Sunday roasts. Immigrants set off in search of freedom and happiness and travel thousands of miles to attain them, only to discover that, for human beings, freedom and happiness are collective conditions. You can't have either in isolation. Unless you have your own place in your own land with your own people where you can love, sleep, live with honour and integrity and wake safely in the morning, whatever liberty and joy you think you have eventually reveals itself as empty. To be happy, you must have a home. Some immigrants manage to make a new one. Many don't. The only mystery is not in why immigrants bundle together in their new lands but why so few of us were aware of this yawning flaw in our plans before we set out.

I found myself meeting up regularly with other Kurds. Since many of us had been dissidents, politics was often high on the agenda. At first, I was suspicious of these oppositions in exile, which seemed to be all talk and little action. But a friend was continually telling me about PJAK, the grandly named Kurdish

Free Life Party in Iran, and the PKK, the Kurdistan Workers Party in Turkey, and its founder Abdullah Öcalan, or Apo.

One day, out of politeness, I asked him to give me the best of Öcalan's many books. He gave me several, a couple of political tracts and a biography. For want of anything better to do, I began reading. The more I read, the more I felt like Apo was making sense of my own life. In Sardasht, my mother had refused to bow to my father and the idea of a male hierarchy. This was how she had forged her freedom. Her rebellion had bred in me an antipathy towards religion, or any state or economy based on ethnic exclusion. This was how I had become a dissident.

But somehow since my arrival in England, I had abandoned my purpose. Maybe I had thought I could be happy with supermarkets and a flat and weekend hiking trips across the moors. And maybe, for a while, I was. But now I saw those things for what they were: distractions. It was like a veil was being lifted. By untangling my past, Apo's words made me see my present for what it was, and set a course for my future. Though I had yet to articulate it, Apo made me realise that there had been an emptiness and uncertainty creeping into my life. With all the stress of escaping from Iran and travelling across Europe, then all the bureaucracy and procedure of asylum and my everyday worries about work and rent and fitting in and making a new life, I had forgotten why I had first set out on this path. Apo was drawing me back to my original purpose. I could feel it filling me like a flood.

In the summer of 2010, a cousin and I took a car and drove south from Leeds. We drove onto the train to France, then on through Belgium, Germany, Austria, Hungary, Serbia and

Bulgaria down to Istanbul, from where we headed east for a thousand miles before dropping into northern Iraq and finally Irbil. For a total of five days and a few hundred pounds in petrol I was retracing the route that six years earlier, in reverse, had taken weeks, risked my life and cost my family thousands of dollars. Such were the privileges of a rich-world passport.

To anyone who asked, my cousin and I were visiting family in and around South Kurdistan. My cousin, in fact, had no other motive. But my intention was to visit the Kurdish revolutionary army in the southern Turkish mountains that, by now, I had been reading about for years. Finding it proved surprisingly easy. I took a bus towards the peaks and climbed ever higher until I came to a checkpoint. Presenting myself to the Kurdish guards, I explained that I had come to see free Kurdistan for myself. By their reaction, they were used to visitors.

'What's your name?' one of them asked.

'Sora,' I said.

The guard laughed. 'Not your real name,' he said, 'your movement name. You need to keep your true identity secret.'

Behind the guards, one of their comrades was wheeling a barrow of tomatoes, potatoes, lemons, garlic and spinach. 'What's your name?' I asked the man.

'Azad,' he replied with a smile.

'Perfect,' I said to the guards. 'My movement name is Azad.'

I travelled on for another few hours until I arrived at a camp. There I was shown to the team with whom I would be staying. The camp was in a stunning position in a valley ringed by towering snowy mountains, carpeted with summer flowers and watered by a river of fast, cold, grey melt-water. I wasn't there for the scenery, however. I wanted to see for myself if Apo's ideas were as inspiring in practice as they were on the page.

I was allowed to wander freely around the camp. Though the

169

volunteers moved every few months, they were well organised. They stuck pipes into the river to channel water to kitchens and shower blocks around the camp. The threat of an attack obliged everyone to carry a gun. The more immediate threat of bombing by Turkish warplanes also meant living quarters were generally built in caves or underground. As well as places to sleep, there were libraries, lecture halls and eating tents furnished with large wooden tables that the comrades had made themselves. Before I arrived, I had wondered about food supplies for so many thousands of people in such a remote place. Now I saw that the camp grew its own vegetables, raised its own animals and managed its environment. Litter was kept to a minimum. Plastics were collected, shovelled into a hole well away from the river and burned. Paper, wood and anything else that could be recycled was kept. Even cigarette butts were collected in old cans.

For a month and a half, the volunteers let me watch, observe and take part in meetings and debates. When they discussed politics, I saw how independent men and women were of each other. There was little cheap, meaningless interaction. Even in the smallest of things, they were honest and friendly. There was something in the way they treated each other, how they talked to one another with respect – the way everyone looked each other in the eye. They were confident and clear in their minds about the values and principles with which they wanted to live. Another thing that impressed me: no one tried to recruit me. They fed me and gave me a bed but otherwise let me witness them and their work and make up my own mind. They even listened to my criticisms.

The hub of camp life was the academies, dedicated to education and discussion. Comrades could propose themselves or others for a course in political theory and they would be accepted if they were judged ready and thirsty for knowledge. The length of the courses was calibrated according to experience and aptitude. After two years in the movement you could apply for a beginners' course, which lasted three months. Every four years after that you could apply for a more advanced level of education, courses that lasted four and a half months, then six months, then nine months, the last of which was reserved for potential generals and commanders. For many, this was their first real education. A few struggled. Many more found the experience thrilling and spiritual.

Perhaps the most important feature of the camps was the equality between men and women. In the West, such equality is often understood in terms of absorbing women into positions or structures previously fashioned by men. The camps were attempting a more fundamental change. While the volunteers ultimately wanted men and women to live together as equals, in order to undo millennia of sexism they separated the two genders into different areas and allowed each complete autonomy to build their own institutions and procedures. Once these were established, men and women could come together as equals to discuss how they might collaborate with each other.

I studied the different camp territories, those areas run by women and those run by men. Mostly women and men organised themselves in similar ways, with command structures, administrations, logistics offices and academies. The point was, they had the freedom to do whatever they wanted. It wasn't about men giving power to women. It was about erasing any role for power in a relationship between men and women and, instead, living alongside each other in mutual respect and dialogue. Walking into a women's area and seeing nothing but women going about every task and duty was to understand how different a world we were trying to create. It was quietly magnificent.

After a while, I realised that one reason I enjoyed the freedom to wander where I liked was that our people had bigger concerns than baby-sitting me. The prospect of war was ever-present. The PKK was fighting in Turkey. PJAK was fighting in Iran. The movement's libraries were decorated with pictures of some of the thousands of Kurds who had died in three decades of struggle. No one doubted there would be more war to come. And there came a moment a few weeks into my stay when I realised that I would be happy to stand beside them. In search of freedom, I had travelled thousands of miles only to circle back almost to where I had started. But now I knew. This was where I belonged. These were my people. Whatever troubles were to come, this was my home.

I returned to Leeds. When Syria erupted in civil war in the spring of 2011, I quit my job as a delivery driver and moved to Sweden to work as a journalist for a Kurdish channel. One day in the summer of 2013, for a report I was preparing, I emailed the Kurdish administration in Qamishli, Rojava, asking for details of the resources they lacked.

Volunteers, they replied.

SEVENTEEN

Kobani,

December 2014 to January 2015

By the end of December we had been fighting in Kobani for four months. The days passed unnoticed in a fog of frozen numbness and fatigue. I had been shooting from the roof of the Black School for more than five weeks and it was becoming hard to remember an existence prior to trudging up and down those stairs, staring out at the same buildings in the same streets. Fighting exhaustion had become so routine that it had bled into an inability to sleep. Every time I curled up on the ground, I prepared myself for hours of wrestling my pinched, nervy body, trying to convince it to rest.

Much of the fighting could be seen from the hills in Turkey across the border. On New Year's Eve, some of the Kurds who had fled the city and who had watched the battles progress street by street began letting off fireworks. Was it a gesture of support? A celebration? With all the journalists also stationed on those hills, training their cameras on us, sometimes it felt like we were gladiators in a circus.

Still, the more surreal and disorientating Kobani became, there were always some comrades you could count on to keep their heads. Travelling to Kobani from Jazaa four months earlier, I'd gone with a small group that included Serhad. To reach Kobani, we had had to hike for several hours over frozen ground, crawl under a border fence, run past a couple of Turkish border patrols, then travel west for hours in an old bus. Serhad had done the entire journey, twenty-four hours without a break, with a fresh gunshot wound in his stomach.

By mid-December, Serhad was fully healed and in command of a group of six young enthusiastic volunteers, whom I nicknamed the Young Wolves. The Wolves were never far from the action. After our latest advance, they were basing themselves in a house to the south of the Black School that looked directly at ISIS' positions. The Wolves, I knew, were energetic and smart, surrounding their positions with broken tiles and glass and sheets of corrugated iron so that they would hear anyone approaching. But they valued their independence and often didn't respond to radio checks. Around 1 a.m. one night, with the temperature around minus five or so, I saw a figure run towards their building. As I shifted my aim to their position, I saw a second figure dart across the street. I was about to fire when I thought better of it and decided to radio Serhad first. When I described what I was seeing, he replied, 'Don't shoot! That's us!' It was a lesson in how I needed to understand our own people as well as I understood the enemy.

A day or so later, around noon and in broad daylight, the jihadis attacked the Wolves' position in full force. Hearing the firefight, I ran over to their base. By the time I arrived, the Wolves had already cut down six Islamists, three right at the doorstep of their base, where their bodies now lay slumped.

The Wolves' base was little more than rubble. There were RPG holes in the walls, and bullets and shrapnel had turned what remained into something approaching a giant sieve. But my comrades were unharmed. I made my way upstairs to find Serhad, who had fashioned a position out of a collapsed staircase. He was sitting stock-still with his neck stretched out and his rifle pointed out through a small hole at the houses across the street. 'Good that you came, Azad,' he said, without lifting his eyes. 'About twenty to twenty-five of them attacked. We killed three in the street and three up against our own wall. There's about fifteen of them left.'

I sat next to him and readied my rifle. Once both of us were still, I realised the jihadis were so close that I could hear them talking.

'There's a guy hiding in the front yard opposite,' Serhad whispered.

I moved my scope to where Serhad was indicating. There was a small copse. Dangling from the branches of the trees were hundreds of strips of cloth, apparently a kind of camouflage meant to simulate leaves.

'The guy has a mask on,' Serhad continued. 'He's moving around, trying to see what's happening. I think he's coordinating the attack, trying to get his men inside our building. He looked right at me two times. But he doesn't fire, as he's trying to hide.'

I told Serhad I couldn't see the man.

'Watch this,' said Serhad.

He fired a single shot.

Something moved. Next to the end of a wall, I could just make out a pair of eyes looking back at us. As I brought my crosshairs down to his head, however, they disappeared.

We lay there, waiting for the man to reappear. After a while, Serhad said, 'I can hear them talking inside that house two blocks over to the left.'

I swung my Dragunov in the building's direction. In a

driveway I saw a man in a YPG uniform peering inside an abandoned jeep as though trying to work out if there was anything in it worth taking. 'YPG or ISIS?' I whispered to Serhad.

Serhad glanced at the man. 'ISIS,' he replied. 'All the comrades are inside.'

I fixed my sights on the man. He was three hundred metres away. It was a clean shot.

One . . .

Two . . .

My bullet hit him in the right lung. He screamed and jumped in the air. His rifle, which he was carrying in his hands, spun backwards and landed on the ground. Somehow, the man landed on his feet.

One . . .

Two . . .

My second shot hit his left lung. He fell backwards onto a pile of rubble.

All around, the Young Wolves were cheering. '*Biji biji Y-P-G! Biji biji Y-P-J!* [Long live YPG! Long live YPJ!]' they shouted.

There was no way for the jihadi to escape. He was in pain, probably dying. We could hear him crying out. Then, as Serhad and I watched, his left arm moved. He seemed to be trying to push himself up. He scrabbled around with his hands until he found two pieces of concrete, then pushed down on them to raise himself up, before finally sitting back on his knees.

Now I could see that my target was a tall, broad-shouldered man in his late thirties. He was tanned, athletic and healthy, with a full head of long black hair and a short beard that he kept neatly trimmed around his thick lips. I had hit him once in either lung, one shot just above his heart, one slightly below it. A small trickle of blood ran from each wound. Beneath his strong arching eyebrows he had calm brown eyes. He was looking directly at me and his expression was composed and unafraid. He knew who he was and what path he had chosen and that he had reached its end. He did not beg. He did not surrender. He accepted his fate. And as I watched this man, proud in death, without fear or regret, I realised that with all that we stood for, all our fine words about conduct and progression and morality, and everything we said about the Islamists' savagery and regression, in that moment I was being taught a lesson in dignity by a jihadi.

I fixed my sights on the point between his two eyebrows. His right arm started to lift his rifle. I moved my finger to my trigger. He raised his weapon until it was almost level. I held his eyes until the last moment.

After it was done, Serhad let me lie there behind my gun for a while.

Then he said, 'The other guy is back,' and fired off a burst. The man went down and we heard a choking sound.

We waited half an hour. A coalition jet flew overhead and fired several rockets into the ISIS positions. We waited some more, then went over to check the bodies. I had hit mine between the eyes. Serhad had shot his through the Adam's apple.

Three weeks later, on the morning of 27 January 2015, we liberated Kobani.

The day before had been an uncertain one. Thick black smoke had hung over the entire front like a dark blanket in the sky. Haqi had radioed around to tell everyone to be prepared. 'They're setting fire to the entire city,' he said. 'It's a full-frontal attack.' I positioned myself in a minaret to protect the teams who were advancing. But my suspicion was that the fires were to cover the jihadis' retreat. The smoke lasted all day. No one

fired at us. Finally, Haqi radioed again. The last surviving jihadis were pulling out of Kobani.

The next morning, one by one, our men and women began
to emerge from their bases and walk through the streets. They
walked to the edge of the city. Covering the teams that I could
see, I watched one walk right through to the outskirts of the city
and into the fields beyond. Then another made it, then another. The city was ours. After watching a fourth team walk clean
out of the city, I radioed Haqi and said I wanted to join them.
'I need to be part of this,' I said. 'I've been dreaming of this
moment. I want to feel how it is to put my feet on the ground.'

'Be my guest,' replied Haqi.

I descended the minaret, slung my rifle on my shoulder and
walked down the middle of a street that I had been watching
and observing for all these months. I felt like I had wings. Some
of our men and women were still checking the last houses for
any remaining ISIS. But most of us just looked at each other.
Around me, comrades were crying. Others were dancing and
singing. There was a lot of shooting in the air. Everywhere I saw
dusty, exhausted faces, long, straggly beards, and red eyes, smiling, laughing and crying at the same time. It was an explosion
of freedom. A documentary crew found Herdem in the street,
his gun slung across his back, reeling with happiness. 'Kobani is
not sad any more,' he proclaimed. 'Kobani's heart is no longer
burning. Kobani can be proud once more and hold her head
high. Let the world witness this day! People of Kobani! We
have claimed our city back!'

A comrade who knew me approached. '*Heval*, you are smiling!' he exclaimed. He was right. I hadn't smiled for months.
I thought about that for days afterwards. In many ways, it was
hard to digest the enormity of what we had achieved. With our
old guns and a few hundred men and women we had stopped

the most ruthless, richest and best-equipped militia in the world. ISIS had terrorised the region, abused the name of God, and murdered, tortured, raped and destroyed for years. Their medieval malevolence had seemed unstoppable. They had called a bluff on all the good in the world. But we had stopped them. Then, step by step, building by building, we had pushed them back. We had broken the spell of ISIS' invincibility and the world could breathe again. It was a new beginning for the Kurds and for the world.

But what price had we paid? We had lost thousands. The jihadis had also left their mark on those of us who survived. They had made us killers. They had forced us to live as animals. They had made us love our friends more fiercely than most human beings can ever know, then forced us to watch them die. I had taken so many lives that I now did it without thinking, sometimes without even remembering. Even if we managed to rebuild Rojava and restore some normality, how could we, the fighters who had saved it, ever be a part of it?

I came across Zahra with a group of volunteers, raising our flag on a hill overlooking the city. As ever, she greeted me with a smile. But for the first time since I had known her, she allowed sadness into her voice. 'I just wish all our friends could have been here to see this day,' she said. 'Only a few days ago I was talking to some of them about what we would do to celebrate. None of them made it to this day. They should be here too.'

I climbed up the tallest building I could find, one of the southernmost in the city. There I put my rifle down, took my jacket off, then my shoes and socks, until I was stripped to the waist, just to feel the openness and the freedom. Our commanders were shouting on the radio: 'Take up positions! Build bases! This is a very important moment! We could be attacked at any time!' But nobody was listening. Everyone was just wandering around and feeling the thrill of liberation. The city echoed with their release.

When I climbed down, I realised I was feeling uneasy. I think part of me was afraid of the celebrations, of letting go of the will and determination that had got us through the past four months. During our training, they had taught us to be wary of the time after a victory. 'You lose more people after a success,' our instructor had said. 'You forget yourselves, you lower your guard and you become vulnerable. Happiness exposes you.' When I ran into a young YPJ fighter from Kobani handing out chocolate and what she called 'the sweets of liberation', I snapped at her. 'We haven't even cleared the city yet,' I reminded her. 'After that there's the villages, the farms, the rest of West Kurdistan, then North and East Kurdistan.'

The woman's face dropped. I immediately regretted my words. 'Come, come,' I said. 'Don't stop. Let's celebrate.'

But she replied, 'No, you are right. We need to liberate more. We need to go on.' And she put away the sweets and walked away.

All afternoon I wandered around the city in a daze. As evening approached, I turned a corner and was stunned to see a family – a mother and her two children who seemed to have chosen the first possible moment to return. They appeared dumbfounded by the devastation around them. So much of what they knew was gone. I could see them struggling to imagine the diabolical forces that had transformed the city into the ruin it now was.

I couldn't help staring back at them. For months I had been crawling through the grey, funereal, frozen dust of the dead. It lay across the city like a shroud. Now here were the colours of life: a mother in a bright-blue traditional Kurdish dress, her children in pink, red and blue silks. I felt like I was looking at a distant memory.

I sat down in a doorway, my rifle across my lap, and watched that family until night fell. My mind had held my heart at bay for so long. Watching this family and others like them, I told myself, was how my heart would begin to repair the space between them.

The day after Kobani's liberation, I had my first shower in months. I warmed the water using an old oil heater in a house we were using, then stood there for what seemed like hours, soaping and washing, soaping and washing. I hadn't felt so clean since swimming in the river outside Sardasht as a boy.

Around noon, a call came over the radio for the snipers to assemble at our base in the city. It was a strange reunion. Herdem, Yildiz, Hayri, Nasrin and I each could have talked for months. Inside my head, it felt so loud. But it was not the time, and if we began with our stories, none of us knew when we would stop. So we just sat silently together, touching each other on the shoulder, peaceful and calm and happy to be in our group of five again.

After a while, Herdem and Yildiz stood and faced us. Of our original seventeen snipers, they said, four were badly wounded, four had lost their minds and one, Servan, was dead. Eight of us had survived, and for us, Herdem said, there would be no let-up. We all needed to return to the war immediately as our forces pushed south from the city into the countryside. 'We have freed the city,' he said. 'But Kobani is in a very weak position. ISIS is waiting outside and they want it back. We need to move to the villages as soon as we can to deny ISIS the space to counter-attack.'

Yildiz added that outside Kobani lay three hundred and seventy-four villages that needed to be recaptured. The terrain would be largely flat. Our new targets would be a series of gently sloping hills that held height advantage over the surrounding area and on which ISIS had built fortified bases. We should expect to encounter these redoubts all the way to the Euphrates to the west and the border of Iraq to the east.

I spoke up. From Jazaa, I had experience of sniping in villages. 'It's mobile, and lots of walking,' I said. 'Not sitting and watching life and death through a hole like we've been doing for the last four months. Now we're going to be able to see the sky. Now we'll have room to roam.'

Everyone laughed at that. I suppose it was funny. But it was also true that we had been living our whole lives through these tiny holes, and our minds had narrowed as a result. It had affected my vision, too. For weeks after Kobani I would find myself spooking people by talking to them with one eye closed, as though I were lining up a shot. Even today I'll walk down a street in London or Leeds and catch myself scanning windows for sniper nests and sizing up passers-by.

I asked to rejoin Haqi and Serhad on the western front, pushing towards the Euphrates, which marked the traditional border of Kurdistan, in whose waters I had begun to dream of washing my face. The others said they were happy to take the eastern and southern fronts. Once our deployments were agreed, we cooked some rice and beans, and ate. It was the last time Herdem, Yildiz, Hayri, Nasrin and I would be together.

EIGHTEEN

Outside Kobani,

January–February 2015

Herdem left as soon as he had finished eating, picking up a pistol and a black Dragunov. A few hours later he returned in a truck, parked, opened the back, hauled out the bodies of nine ISIS fighters, dragged them to the side of the road and lined them up in sequence.

I learned later that Herdem had walked straight from our meeting to a village three kilometres beyond our frontline where he knew ISIS were repositioning. There he'd crept up to a house inside which he could see the enemy and started firing through the windows – shooting, ducking down, popping up at another window, then shooting again. As the jihadis panicked inside, thinking they were surrounded, Herdem took his time. In ten minutes, he cut all nine of them down. Then he heaved their bodies onto their truck and drove it back to the city.

Part of me understood. On one of the last nights before we retook Kobani, he and I had teamed up for an assault on one of the remaining sets of buildings still in ISIS' hands. We were watching a street in which several teams had positioned themselves. The opposite side was controlled by ISIS. I took first watch. When Herdem relieved me, I was in the middle of showing him our positions when I was interrupted by another commander, who took over my briefing.

At around 2 a.m., Herdem saw the top of a man's head pop up behind a wall of sandbags on the balcony of a house on the ISIS side of the street, around two hundred metres away. Not wanting to miss the shot, he fired immediately. After just seconds, the radio exploded with the news that one of our most popular commanders, Hamza, was down. I went to check. There was so much blood it looked like ten men had been hit. The trajectory of the single bullet that had passed through Hamza's neck suggested it came from our lines. When I found the hole where the round had burrowed into the wall, I dug into the brick and pulled out an M16 slug. There was no doubt that this was Herdem's shot.

Herdem was devastated. His distress was exacerbated by the men in Hamza's units, who loved their commander and immediately ostracised Herdem, declaring they would never fight with him again and asking him to stay away from their positions.

Herdem blamed himself, of course. But over the next few days I watched as his agony turned to rage at everything ISIS had done to him. Hamza's death, the death of Herdem's friends, the destruction of the city and all the years of killing – none of it would have happened were it not for ISIS. Herdem had been fighting for his people and for a cause. Look what they made him do! Look what they made him into! From then on, I think he decided he would be fighting to show ISIS what they had created.

Herdem was also displaying the same wholly unnatural absence of caution that many of us were exhibiting. We had begun to feel untouchable. Fear, in the end, is about what you don't know, and Herdem, I and the others had made such a study of the colours and forms of death that it was impossible to be scared of it any more. Over the next few weeks I would hear story after story about how Herdem was attacking villages and hills single-handedly, killing every ISIS fighter he found. I was even told that one day he shot two ISIS fighters then, to keep warm that night, bedded down between them.

Because I spoke English, Herdem asked me to chaperone a volunteer from Hungary called Zuli. At forty-seven, Zuli's burning ambition to kill a few ISIS fighters had persuaded him to leave his job as a nurse in Budapest, say goodbye to his wife, three daughters and two sons, and travel to the war. 'It was when I heard the news that ISIS were raping women and killing children and beheading people,' he told me. 'I had to do something about it.' Zuli was good company. But his anger troubled us. 'Try to keep him back from the front,' Tolin told me. 'If you find a way to let him kill a few of them safely, let him do it and then maybe he'll go back to his family.'

Herdem drove Zuli and me outside the city to a village called Selim, west of Kobani, where Haqi was stationed. 'ISIS has mined everything,' said Herdem. 'Don't ever walk in the fields. Don't even think of visiting the graveyards. Stay on the roads. Our de-miners have cleared the roads.'

We arrived in Selim to find Haqi in an old radio station building, making a fire and planning an attack that night. The village was in a valley. ISIS were about two kilometres away on a hill to the west. They were harassing our positions, advancing to a group of fifteen houses between our two fronts, firing their Kalashnikovs and RPGs, then retreating again. Haqi and I agreed we should take these houses first. To assist the advance,

I would crawl to within a few hundred metres to scout the target and provide cover.

I spent the evening creating a camouflage suit by pulling the threads out of empty farmers' sacks and sewing the tassels onto my clothes. I set off at 3 a.m., crouching and elbowing my way forward until I was a hundred metres from the target houses. I couldn't move or shoot as I would be discovered. My job was to stay hidden and count how many jihadis there were and which of the houses they were using. I stayed in the frozen mud all night and all the next day, stock-still, observing, pissing in my clothes, even watching a jihadi drop his trousers and take a crap. After sixteen hours, I was sure there were nine of them. When ISIS returned to their main base for the night, I radioed Haqi and he sent up a group of volunteers who took over the vacant houses without a fight.

It was just as well that they didn't need me. I was more tired than ever. Inside one of the houses the next day I was eating a piece of warmed cheese and drinking a glass of tea when a bullet came through the window and slapped into the wall behind me. Chilled to the bone and stiff as a board, I wasn't sure I could have moved even if I'd wanted to. The team commander apparently felt the same and, like me, remained at the table, eating and sipping his tea. A second bullet hit the wall behind us. Then a third. Eventually, I picked up my rifle, walked out through the back door, sighted up the ISIS position a kilometre away and, noticing an anomalous black shadow inside a hay manger, fired. The black spot disappeared and the shooting stopped.

As we advanced west, we came across two villages in ISIS' hands, Big and Little Boban, and, to the south, a smooth and gradual rise called Sûsan Hill, where commander Cudi had been run over by a tank five months earlier. Our plan was to take Little Boban and Sûsan Hill, then fire down on Big Boban from both positions and force ISIS to retreat. We always tried to leave the jihadis a way out. This meant we might have to fight them again, but our priority was always taking back our land, not killing.

With the help of a few coalition air strikes, we took Sûsan Hill without a fight. Around 4 a.m. the next day, I left Zuli and advanced alone to a small clump of trees to observe Little Boban. If there were only three or four jihadis, my idea was to take them out myself. Around 8.30 that morning I saw two figures set out on foot from one of the houses. Ten minutes later, another five followed them. An eighth man on a motorbike came and left, presumably delivering orders. The jihadis on foot were striding purposefully with long, firm steps, not stopping or looking back, and carrying several spare bags of ammunition. I was sure I was watching the start of a counter-attack on Sûsan Hill.

I snuck back the way I had come, called Haqi, relayed my observations, then set out across the fields for Sûsan Hill. It was heavy going, soft and muddy. At one point I was challenged by a woman's angry voice on the radio: 'Who is walking in the fields alone?'

'Azad,' I replied. 'I'm a sniper. I'm always alone.'

The woman was a commander called Golan. She told me she had been listening in to ISIS' radio and heard them say that our fighters were fleeing Sûsan Hill.

'I'm not running away,' I shouted. 'I'm coming towards you!'

Before we had time for more disagreement, ISIS began shooting at me from their positions around two kilometres away. A round hit the earth near my feet, then another. From the sound,

I could tell the jihadis were using a BKC, a large-calibre Dushka and a Kalashnikov or two. A BKC or a Kalashnikov could kill with a single round and a Dushka would cut me in two. But none of them were accurate over distance. I kept walking. I had little choice: the mud was too sticky for running. After a few more steps, without really thinking what I was doing, I stopped, turned to face my attackers, opened my arms wide, closed my eyes, and just stood there. *I won't be hit*, I told myself. *I can't be hit.* Several bullets slapped the earth around me. After a while, I lowered my arms, opened my eyes, turned back in the direction I had been headed and trudged on. The jihadis seemed to give up and the bullets stopped. It felt like I had proved something, though what, and to whom, I wasn't sure.

I made it to a cluster of houses at the foot of Sûsan Hill in the thick of the midday heat, took a seat on a doorstep and caught my breath. To the east were my comrades. To the west was ISIS. The summit of Sûsan Hill was our frontline dividing the two. There were four comrades in two shallow foxholes on the top of the hill, trying to hold out against the ISIS counter-attack. I walked around the back of the hill and made it to a group of our fighters who were providing cover fire for the foxholes. 'Most of the guys out on the hill are just new arrivals,' warned one. 'Never been in battle before.'

Fzzz! Fzzz!

We pressed our faces into the dirt as bullets flew over our heads. In the distance, I could hear a Dushka starting up. I drained a bottle of water which the others had passed to me and, when I felt a pause in the fire, set off up the hill for the first foxhole. As I was running up, I saw one of our men, a teenager, running down towards me. As we passed each other, I grabbed him by his collar, flipped him onto his back, dragged him back into the hole and stuck my knee on his chest.

'What are you doing?' I shouted. 'Nobody is leaving! This is where Cudi fought and died. So will we if we have to! Nobody leaves here as long as I'm alive!'

In the foxhole was a second man, bleeding from the head. I looked at the teenager under my knee. He looked scared half to death, though now perhaps more of me than ISIS. The enemy fire was intensifying, thumping into the ground around us. I rolled off the boy, pressed my body into the foxhole, all of half a metre deep, and waited for the next pause in the fusillade.

After a minute or so, with no sign of a break in incoming fire, I jumped up and ran the twenty metres to the second, higher foxhole, skidding in next to two comrades and an old, broken BKC covered in dirt and blood. One of the two, another young man, was screaming into his radio: 'We're surrounded! They're everywhere! We need to leave!'

I reached over and turned off his radio. 'You can't talk like that,' I told him. 'You'll scare people.'

The second comrade, in his late twenties, was calmer. Registering my Dragunov, he anticipated my purpose. 'There are five on that hill six hundred metres away to the right,' he told me. 'Two are creeping up towards us behind that low wall over there four hundred metres to the front. Three more are in the houses down the hill five hundred metres to the far left. And there are three Dushkas, on the right, on the left and straight ahead on the far side of the valley, all out of our range. In the foxhole you came from, one comrade was hit in the head by shrapnel kicked up by a Dushka round.'

'Got it,' I said.

I zeroed my scope to six hundred and fifty metres. To the right, I could see the five jihadis. They were standing together

189

out in the open, as casual as cowboys, with their forward feet resting on rocks as they shot at us. I fired at them, once, then again. It was like a grenade had gone off. All five threw themselves to the ground and took cover behind a small rise.

'Watch them with your binoculars,' I said to my spotter. 'I'll scan the other side.'

I switched to the wall running up the hill. As my comrade had said, there were two ISIS men crouching behind it, edging towards us. One was carrying a BKC. I went for him. He went down, though I couldn't tell if I'd hit him or whether he was taking cover.

Next were the houses at the base of the hill. On the roof of one was a guy firing a BKC from the hip. I hit him in the chest. He flipped over backwards, somersaulting off the roof as though he was doing a backwards dive.

It was suddenly much quieter. There was still the occasional *fzzz* of an incoming round but the barrage had stopped for now. I took the chance to adjust my position in the foxhole, pull my camo over myself and reload my magazine.

'Nobody is leaving,' I insisted.

The jihadis soon recovered and restarted their attack. Just when the incoming fire seemed to reach a new pitch, I felt it veer off to my right. I looked around to see the two youngsters from the other foxhole lying outside it on the ground, their faces in the dirt. They'd tried to make another run for it, then come under fire and thought better of it. Bullets were kicking up dust all around them. They weren't dead yet, but death was one well-aimed shot away.

'Stand up!' I shouted at them. 'Stand up!'

I grabbed a large stone and threw it at the nearer man, hitting him in the back. Startled, he looked round at me.

Enunciating as clearly as I could above the noise of the bullets, I said, 'Pick up the wounded man and take him to the back. I will give you cover.'

The young man nodded and got to his feet. I began firing in rapid succession, two quick shots to the left, two more at the wall, two more at the houses. I was through my mag in seconds. I reloaded a second, then a third. Behind me, my two comrades were shuffling away slowly towards cover. I shouted at the teenager in my foxhole to take the ammunition belt off the BKC, clean the dirt and blood off the bullets, then load them into my spare mags. I kept firing. In my left hand, I could feel my barrel overheating. I was down to my last thirty rounds.

'I need gun oil and more Dragunov rounds,' I shouted into my radio.

As I reloaded once more, I lifted my rifle to my eye to begin firing again when it flew out of my hands. My scope hit me in the eye, knocking me back and into the dirt. It felt like my eye had been ripped from my skull. I put my fingers to my face. My eyelid was closed but my eyeball was still there.

I prised my eyelid open with my thumb and forefinger, trying to blink back the rising bruise. My rifle was behind me. Next to it was a large white stone, shattered into pieces. I could read what had happened: a heavy-calibre bullet had hit the stone, knocked it into my barrel, and the force of the collision had ripped the weapon from my hands and smashed it into my face.

I checked the Dragunov. The scope was fine. Aside from a scrape on the barrel and some peeling paint due to the overheating, the gun was also functional. So was I.

*

By now, I had been shooting at a steady pace for more than an hour. During a lull, a comrade skidded past and dropped off more gun oil and a big box of ammunition, including some armour-piercing rounds. The two men in the foxhole with me kept me supplied. I tried to slow my shots, firing only when I saw movement. Another hour passed. I noticed the enemy's Dushka had gone quiet, either broken or out of bullets.

I was so focused on the battle in front of me that the first I knew of Janiwar's presence was when I heard a clanking metal sound behind me. I looked back to see him working on the old Dushka. 'If we can get this thing working,' he said, 'we'll hold them off easily.'

Suddenly he screamed and fell on me. 'I've been hit in the leg!' he cried. 'They shot my leg.'

I looked at his wound. He was bleeding but it didn't seem life-threatening. 'It's just your leg, comrade,' I said. I grabbed his scarf and threw it at him so he could make a tourniquet.

Janiwar went quiet, tying his scarf tightly around his leg to stop the bleeding. Once he was satisfied, he looked up. 'Azad,' he said, 'you fire at the enemy and I'll run back.'

'That's it?' I asked. 'You come, you get wounded and you leave?'

I was only teasing. But Janiwar grimaced.

'Three, two, one, GO!' I shouted.

But as Janiwar got to his feet, I realised I'd made a mistake: my rifle was empty. 'STOP!' I shouted. 'Duck back down – I'm out!'

Janiwar scrambled back into the foxhole. I could see he wanted to hit me in the face. But he controlled himself and watched me reload. When I was done, he said, 'Test it first. And this time, I'll count it off.'

I fired a shot.

Janiwar nodded. 'Three, two, one, GO!'

I fired two shots left, two centre, two more right, then repeated until I finished the mag. For a moment, the battlefield was deadly quiet. I looked over at my spotter. He caught my eye and nodded at the younger comrade squatting next to me.

The teenager was huddled in a ball, his arms around his knees, his face in his hands. Sticky dark blood was pouring through his fingers. It had already made a deep, dark pool in his lap and was spilling onto the ground around him.

'Tie his wound!' I shouted.

'I can't!' the other man shouted back. 'He's been hit in the mouth. He would choke.'

'Press some cloth on it and take him back,' I said.

I waited until they were ready, then counted them off.

'Three, two, one . . .'

I knelt up and started firing once more. Beside me, my spotter pulled the boy's arm over his shoulder, lifted him to his feet and began walking him across the hill. They went slowly, the older man heaving the younger one along, leaving a trail of dragged feet and blood in the dust. Eventually, they disappeared down the hill. Later, Janiwar told me that the bullet that had hit his leg was the same one that had passed through the boy's mouth then out of his neck.

It was 4 p.m. by now. My comrades had left me. I realised ISIS was departing too. Down the hill to the right I could see one jihadi helping a wounded man off the battlefield. The two behind the wall were either dead or had left. The group on the cluster of houses to the left had moved back a few hundred metres into the valley. It was the first time I had seen ISIS retreat with my own eyes. But I was in no mood for mercy.

My comrade had been hit in the mouth. Another had been hit in the leg, and another in the head. I'd nearly lost an eye. Whenever I spotted the jihadis, I fired. I dropped one more at a thousand metres. Then I jumped up out of the foxhole and began running down the hill towards them, firing as I went.

'Wait! Wait!' came a voice on my radio. 'Where are you going?'

The voice steadied me. I walked back up the hill, rejoined my comrades, and together we descended the hill to make sure the jihadis were gone. I found the bodies of at least two that I had hit. The guy I had shot on the roof was a mess: my bullet had knocked a wad of white fat out through his back and onto his vest, as though squeezed from a tube of toothpaste. Over to the right was another dead jihadi who was wearing new leather zip-up boots. I was pleased to see that one of my rounds had hit him in the foot and the blood had ruined the silk lining.

Of all the engagements I fought, Sûsan Hill remains the one of which I am most proud. Cudi had died for that hill. Outnumbered ten to one, with only a rifle against BKCs and Dushkas, I'd used my Dragunov like a machine gun to hold it. When I left the foxhole, it was filled with more than a thousand bullet casings. The camouflage paint on the barrel was all burned off. For days afterwards, my shoulder was purple and yellow with the bruising from the recoil. But they hadn't taken Sûsan Hill. With Cudi beside me, they hadn't come close.

NINETEEN

Southwest of Kobani,

March 2015

As we moved south and east, our lines widened and thinned, and we found ourselves working in ever smaller groups. After the confines of Kobani, this new spread-out war threw up some surprises. Haqi, who came from the area, began asking families he knew to return from Turkey to the north, saying they were needed to fill the gaps in our forces in case the jihadis tried to slip over the border and attack us from behind. One day I came across a man with a long beard in black clothes with a gun in his hands and raised my rifle at him, only for him to address me in Kurdish. He had responded to Haqi's request and returned from Turkey but hadn't stopped to consider how his appearance might describe him.

As we advanced, we managed to solve some of the mysteries of what had happened to our men and women who disappeared in the first days of the ISIS attack. One morning we found seven of their bodies lying next to each other in a room in an abandoned house. All had been executed with a single bullet to the head. Their bodies were lying where they had fallen. The exposed parts of their flesh were turning to parchment. The skin on their faces was drawn back over their bones as tight as stretched leather. When we tried to lift them to take them back to Kobani to be buried, they fell apart in our arms. The smell of putrefaction was unbearable. Several of us vomited. Eventually, we gathered their body parts into some old grain sacks, tied them up and carried them out.

The new distances between us and the enemy also gave the jihadis a chance to try fresh forms of deception. A few weeks after the battle at Sûsan Hill, we came across another gently sloping incline called Qeregoyê. On it was a farmhouse and several outbuildings in which our commanders said a large group of Islamists were making a stand, holding up our entire advance. I volunteered to scout the farmhouse and crawled forward behind a small stone wall until I was three hundred metres away. Through my scope, I saw one of the Islamists throw a bottle of water down to a small shed that was the jihadis' most forward position. A few minutes later, another figure ran across the top of the hill behind the main house. Then a third sprinted down to a small barn to the side, ferrying a pillow to be used as a sandbag. A fourth appeared carrying a blanket. Then a fifth came into view ferrying a mattress. There had to be at least ten of them, I thought.

I radioed Haqi and Golan. 'We need an air strike,' I said. 'There's a lot of them and they're digging in.'

As I was talking, however, another figure made a dash across some open ground and I realised I had seen this man before, or at least part of him: he was wearing the same jacket as one I had seen further up the hill. Now that I knew what to look for, each time a jihadi made another run, I focused on the jacket. It was the same jacket every time. I realised I had been looking at the same man all along.

'You know what?' I called Haqi and Golan again. 'It's only

one guy. He's faking the whole thing. He's pretending to be resupplying a force of ten people or so. But he's the only one moving.'

'We're bringing up the tank,' Haqi replied.

Our 'tank' was actually an old Toyota fitted with heavy metal plates to cover its sides and tyres. It took fifteen minutes to reach me. As it clanked past, the men and women inside opened fire, then advanced to the farmhouse firing continuously, at which point five of our fighters jumped out of the back and stormed inside. I joined them and we repeated the manoeuvre for each of the outbuildings. We met no resistance in any of them.

The jihadi in the jacket was lying on the ground in front of the farmhouse, his head split open by a Dushka round. There was a second ISIS fighter nearby who had been hit seven or eight times in his stomach and legs and who might have been dead for some time. A third body was inside one of the outbuildings. And that was it. Three jihadis against one hundred of us – and they had held us off all day. War is often imagined like a great battle scene in a movie where dozens of extras are wiped out at once. In real life, there are no extras in war. Everyone gets to play a central character.

Out of habit, I inspected the third body. The corpse was lying on the floor, and from the size of the torso, it was the body of a boy, perhaps thirteen or fourteen. He was wearing blue jeans but was otherwise stripped to the waist, revealing his pale-pink skin. There was a terrible smell in the room. When I walked around the body, I realised the boy's face was lying in a smouldering fire. Most of his features had been burned off. On and around him were magazines of bullets. Some of the rounds were still exploding.

I grabbed him and started to drag him out of the fire. A comrade shouted at me to stop: the boy was dead and it might be a booby-trap. I felt in the boy's pockets. There were no papers. There was a mobile phone next to him but it had nothing on it – no music, no pictures – except three local numbers and a detailed military map of the area. We never found out any more about this boy. Who was he? A Russian? A Chechen? A European? Why had his fellow jihadis taken such trouble to obscure his features? Perhaps he was important. Perhaps he wasn't. What struck me was the gruesomeness with which the jihadis had erased any hint of his earthly identity. *There is nothing we won't do in this world*, they seemed to be saying. *None of what happens here matters.*

War had levelled Kobani, turning it into a hot, dry Dresden. Out in the villages, however, we were met not so much by the ruins of war as the absence of life. Our people had abandoned their homes. Then the jihadis had looted everything they'd left behind. There wasn't a sheep or chicken that had escaped ISIS' kitchens. They stole cooking oil, grain, rice, flour, cheese, tea and even the kettles and glasses that went with them. They pilfered dried grapes, urns of honey and sacks of salted pistachios. They took cars, tractors, petrol, diesel and generators. They forced farmers they captured to pick the olives off their ancient trees. They even stole donkeys to carry away their loot, and guard-dogs to protect it. It was remarkable, really, how even as we began to understand that the war for Rojava was in its final few months, ISIS' band of rapists, murderers, thieves and thugs would offer us new outrages to renew our fury.

One of our last objectives was the village of Misko, a place of several hundred houses surrounded by rolling hills and a scattering of smaller settlements a day's walk east from the Euphrates. From some of these hills you could see the greenness

of the marsh banks running either side of the great river, perhaps ten or fifteen kilometres away. Misko was too big and well
defended for our hundred or so men and women to capture
immediately, so our plan was to whittle our way in by taking
all the villages that surrounded it one by one, then close in on
Misko from all sides.

It was in one of these villages that, to settle a dispute between returning farmers by appealing for unity in the face of
a common enemy, I told the story of Sûsan Hill. In an aside, I
said I assumed the young fighter who was hit in the mouth had
died of his injuries. After the farmers dispersed, a man came
over to me and introduced himself as Mohandis, an engineer.

'This wounded guy is not dead,' he said.

'I want to believe you, brother,' I replied. 'But he lost so
much blood.'

'No,' said Mohandis. 'I *know* he's not dead. I know his sister.
We're from the same village. I spoke to her just now.'

'Can you call her?' I asked.

He could. A few seconds later, a woman was telling me on
Mohandis' phone that she had just returned from Turkey where
she had visited her injured brother in hospital. Her father was
still with him, she said, and she gave me the number. When we
phoned her father, the man told me his son was unconscious in
intensive care and, looking through the glass, he described his
boy to me. 'Big thick brown eyebrows, brown skin, not too tall.
Shot in the mouth on Sûsan Hill. He can't talk but the doctor
says he may be able to in the future. But he is alive.'

'You don't know what you are giving me,' I said. During the
battle for Sûsan Hill, I had had no thought for anything but
fighting. From the moment the adrenalin subsided, however, I
had been haunted by how I had forced this boy to remain in the
battle. The image of his blood pouring out of his mouth and

welling in his hands had become my new nightmare. He hadn't even been able to call out. He might have died right next to me and I wouldn't have noticed.

'When he wakes up, tell him Azad called,' I said to the father. 'The sniper in the foxhole. Tell him that I am overjoyed that he is alive.'

The man promised to do so. Then he said he had a request for me. 'My house in the village,' he said. 'Can you check that the Islamists are not stealing everything from me?'

It was early spring in South Kurdistan but that February brought the heaviest rain anyone could remember. The downpour lasted a month. The villagers explained it by saying Nature was reminding us that nothing man-made, not even war, could match its power. Our men and women found the weather sapped as much of their strength as the fighting. On the fourth consecutive night of rain I went to visit a team who had been out in the open since it started. Shortly after I left, the commanders decided to move forward. As this team entered a house, the first shelter they had experienced in four days, five of them were killed by a landmine. A few days later another three were badly wounded by an RPG.

I felt that I might help prevent some of these deaths if I had a night scope: my previous one had been requisitioned by another unit weeks earlier. I radioed Herdem to request a new one. But Herdem wasn't available and my call was answered by a junior comrade.

'He is wherever the front is moving forward,' the comrade said. 'He goes and takes over villages and hills, then leaves and goes to another attack.' The man on the other end sounded worried. He described Herdem as exhausted but relentless. 'He kills any jihadi he finds. In one attack, he shot forty-five ISIS single-handedly.'

The man's words made me so sad. It was too much, even for Herdem. He had lost so many friends. He was consumed by a killing rage.

A day or so later, I managed to speak to him on the radio.

'I need a thermal,' I said.

'We only have one and you will need to find an M16 on which to mount it,' he told me. 'But I will send it.'

'Are you OK?' I asked.

'Am I OK?'

'I heard about what you've been doing.'

Herdem was quiet.

'Even if you kill a thousand ISIS, it will not equal one drop of Hamza's blood,' I said. 'I understand how you feel. When I wounded Alisher, I nearly collapsed. But it can happen to anyone.'

I could hear Herdem breathing heavily.

'Maybe take a break,' I said. 'Maybe get some rest back at the sniper base for a few days.'

'How can I rest?' he replied. 'How can I send you to the front and rest back at headquarters?'

I had no answer for him. Herdem repeated that he would send the thermal.

There was a silence.

'If you have anything else you need to say, I am listening,' I said.

'Likewise,' he said. 'If you have anything you need to say, I am listening too.'

'Success, Herdem,' I said, finally.

'Success, Azad.'

*

After a few weeks in the rain and cold, General Golan gave us a new target: Haroon Hill. This tall mass of bare rock, one of the last pieces of high ground before the Euphrates, was named after one of our social workers who had lived and worked there, and who had picked up a gun when ISIS invaded and died there. The hill was more of a mountain, a giant plinth of rock several hundred metres tall. With two ISIS positions on the summit, Golan said Haroon Hill was all but untakeable by ground troops alone. The coalition had agreed to continual air strikes, day and night. We would stand back and watch and, when we were sure the jihadis had all either died or fled, we would take the hill unopposed.

It was a strange sensation to sit back and watch your war being fought in front of you. For ten days, the warplanes bombarded the hill. They were using their most powerful missiles, which would send clouds of dust hundreds of metres into the air. Again and again the bombers came. Underneath the explosions, we would see the Islamists scurrying around like ants under boiling water. Most were enveloped in the dust. More than one seemed to just disappear − a tiny black figure fleeing the bombs one second, nothing there the next. But somehow the survivors managed to keep their black-and-white flag flying.

During a break in the bombardment, I saw nine ISIS fighters emerge from their base and walk down the hill. At first, I couldn't understand it. After enduring the bombing for a week, they were just leaving? I watched them as they strolled over a rise until, one by one, they all disappeared. No more came and there was no movement, not in their base and not in the rocks to the side. When I looked again, however, I realised their base flag was still up.

'They're pretending,' I radioed to Haqi. 'They never forget their flag. It's a very spiritual thing for them. They're trying to make it look like they're retreating but they're preparing to fight. It's a trap.'

Haqi agreed I should go forward and check. Sure enough, I spotted a group of Islamists hiding out in a small cluster of houses down the back of the hill, spread out so as to avoid the air strikes. I radioed to Haqi what I had seen. That night the bombers came again, this time targeting the houses and hillside where I had seen the jihadis. After that, a drone kept circling the area, looking for survivors to pick off. Finally, Serhad went forward with his team. Within an hour he called back to say he had taken the hill without firing a shot.

I joined Serhad on the summit just as dawn broke on the horizon. Behind the ISIS base were four small graveyards. In the first, there were four fully completed graves. The next contained another three graves which were half-dug: the bodies were mostly buried though only a thin scattering of earth had been thrown over the top. Here and there arms and legs protruded. One of the jihadis' faces was showing. To me, he looked as though he was still alive, pretending to be dead. I watched him for a full minute, my rifle to his head and my hand over his mouth to check if he was breathing.

In the third set of graves, two bodies were lying in shallow scoops on the ground. What covering they had seemed to have been thrown over them by the force of an explosion. A toe was sticking out of one small mound of earth. I felt it. Cold. Finally, I came across a pile of corpses and body parts lying out in the open, the remains of perhaps seven or eight people. At least three of them had white skin and ginger hair.

More fighters from the Caucasus, I assumed.

From what I was seeing, an air strike had hit the initial group of jihadis. Another team had come up to bury them and take their places, then another strike had hit them. So a third team had arrived, and a third strike had killed them. Finally, a fourth team had taken over and they had been killed too. It was terrible tactics. It also made no sense to travel all the way from Chechnya or Georgia and fight for so many months and years only to hurl yourself into death. The only possible answer was that they always knew they were going to die, and they welcomed it.

Even then, looking at their bodies, maimed and burned and ripped apart, you had to wonder whether they had thought it through. This didn't look heroic. It looked agonising, stupid and pointless, like some horrific misunderstanding. Maybe they had made a mistake. Maybe they had been misled. Maybe they were just fools. After all, there were easier, more commendable ways to commit suicide than trying to enslave a land and its people. Their sacrifice didn't justify their crimes. It just made them even more blinkered and narcissistic. I wondered whether, in the moment of their death, they had experienced enlightenment at last. But when I studied them, nothing in their blank, frozen expressions suggested illumination – quite the opposite. I have to think that they died dumb.

TWENTY

Close to the Euphrates,

March–April 2015

As the war continued, we inevitably made more mistakes of our own. One evening Serhad and his unit advanced on a village that had not been cleared and, to fool ISIS into thinking they were camping somewhere else, lit a fire, then bedded down a few hundred metres away. When a second group of comrades arrived, they saw the fire and assumed Serhad had checked the area for jihadis before warming himself. So they lit their own blaze and settled in around it. Several more units did the same. In the morning, a comrade called Jamal was stoking the embers to warm himself in the dawn cold when he looked up and, speechless, watched one, two, then three jihadis run out of a house not ten metres away and disappear.

Another time, we took over a small village on a road leading directly towards ISIS' lines to the west. Our Hungarian volunteer Zuli still hadn't fired a shot in anger, the village was easy to defend and I had other places to go, so I placed him on the roof of the last house in the village and told him to shoot anything that came towards him. A small group of new volunteers also took up position on either side of the road.

I returned in the evening to find Zuli in a state of high distress, pushing the other volunteers around, looking like he was going to hit someone.

'This guy wouldn't let me kill him!' he shouted when he saw me. 'I had him right in my sights and they wouldn't let me shoot!'

Between outbursts, Zuli told me that a lone motorbiker with a long beard, dressed in black and wearing a *thawb*, had approached from the west. Zuli was convinced the man was ISIS and was about to shoot when the volunteers called to him that the man might be one of ours. The motorbiker came to a stop. The volunteers shouted across to him, asking for his name and unit. At which point the motorbiker turned around and sped off back in the direction he had come. They showed me the tyre marks. The jihadi had been ten metres away from Zuli.

'You're lucky he didn't steal your tea!' I exclaimed. 'Zuli – why didn't you get him?'

'I did!' cried Zuli. 'I fired again and again but I couldn't hit him.'

I examined Zuli's rifle. His scope was zeroed to a thousand metres. The bullets would have passed clean over the jihadi's head.

I thought the incident was hilarious. For days afterwards I made fun of Zuli, making the sound of a revving motorbike. Zuli didn't think it was funny.

It was during the same advance to the west that Serhad, Jamal, a commander called Dado and I walked into Chargle, a place of forty to fifty mud-walled, tin-roofed houses which turned out to be Haqi's ancestral village. We were half-expecting to run into ISIS. Instead, in a room in a deserted house we found an Aladdin's Cave of supplies. Boxes of ammunition and RPGs, sleeping bags and rain ponchos, American-made backpacks, socks, cots and blankets. In the corridor outside we found a small mountain of fresh food in takeaway containers: meat, onions, orange juice, cakes, pistachios, biscuits, rice, plus gas cookers and piles of spare cylinders.

It could have been poisoned, of course. The thought of taking from ISIS was also unpalatable. Nor had we finished checking the houses for stray jihadis. But we were famished. We lit a stove, found a large pot and threw in some boiled rice, onions, tomatoes, steak and chicken to warm it, then flipped it all out onto a large tray. We must have eaten a kilo each. The feeling in my stomach was one of shock and surprise – it gurgled for days afterwards – and it took all the willpower we had not to stretch out afterwards in the middle of a warzone and take a nap.

ISIS left other gifts. Not far away, I forced the door into the backyard of another house to find a brand-new Honda motorbike with the keys in the ignition. *It has to be booby-trapped*, I thought. I checked the stand, the engine, the seat and the tyres but found nothing. I threw my leg over the seat, turned the key and kick-started it. It was fine. Jamal, who had more experience with bikes, suggested he steer on the muddy roads and I hop on the back. I gathered up a box of RPGs and another of ponchos to take back to our forces and we rode out of the village back up Haroon Hill.

'Can you believe we ate ISIS' food?' shouted Jamal over his shoulder. 'I thought your principles wouldn't have allowed you to swallow!'

I was about to answer when, in front of us, I saw a fishing line running across the road. I quickly traced it to the right-hand side, where there was nothing, then followed it to the left, where there was a large gas cylinder sitting on the verge. Jamal was changing into a higher gear. I grabbed him, trying to pull him down onto the road. But as I gripped him, I saw the bike's front wheel hit the wire.

I released Jamal and threw my arms in the air. Finally, my moment had come. I felt the wild grip of death. An image of my mother flashed into my mind, and another of my home-town, Sardasht, and the waterfall and the green beauty of the countryside. I saw Jazaa. I saw Kobani. I was at peace.

After a while, I realised I could hear somebody's voice. It sounded quiet and distant. I opened my eyes. I was on the back of the bike. It was Jamal talking.

'It didn't explode!' I screamed at him. 'It didn't explode!'

'What?' replied Jamal, braking hard and dropping the bike into the dirt.

I grabbed him by the hand and we ran back the way we had come.

'Where?' demanded Jamal.

One hundred and fifty metres behind us, the large gas cylinder attached to the fishing line was now lying in the road. As we ap-proached, I saw that the other end of the line was tied to a stick that was also lying flat on the ground. We had burst through the trip-wire but instead of tightening it and triggering the detona-tor, the stick holding it taut had popped clean out of the muddy ground. We had cursed the rain for weeks. Now it had saved us.

After a month, we finally took the last village surrounding Misko. We were now able to attack it from the north, south and east, squeezing the jihadis out through a gap running to the west. We wanted to give them an alternative to fighting to the last man, but we wouldn't let them run unmolested. Serhad and his men would cut them down as they went.

I took up a position about a thousand metres out to the southeast, driving the jihadis to the west. I quickly shot dead three of them. It seemed to energise the others. I could hear them shouting and screaming '*Allahu Akbar! Allahu Akbar!*' as they ran into the middle of Misko.

After a few minutes, Serhad called me: 'Azad! Come here! There's a lot of ISIS here.'

I made my way towards him. Serhad was on the roof of a house on the eastern outskirts, ready to attack.

'They're just behind that wall over there,' said Serhad. 'One of them is close.'

I surveyed the wall through my sights. As I did so, a jihadi stood up in full view five hundred metres away. I shot him as he was walking.

Serhad told me he wanted to take over the houses that stood between us and ISIS. When he called Haqi and Golan, however, they requested him to wait for reinforcements. Serhad just switched off his radio.

'Let's do it ourselves, Azad,' he said. 'You cover me. The generals can wait for us this time.'

I reasoned Serhad was going to attack with or without me. 'OK,' I said.

I watched Serhad creep towards the jihadis. As he reached a house, two men stood up and ran behind him. I shot one immediately. He went down screaming, dragging himself behind a rock, his free hand trying to stop the blood pumping from his neck. I moved to his friend and shot him as well. I couldn't help but enjoy it – the skill, the success. I'd become so used to killing that I felt no hesitation, just the feeling of a debate long since settled and a necessary job done.

I spotted two more ISIS nearby and another further away, moving fast. 'Don't move!' I radioed to Serhad. 'Don't go any further! They look like they're about to make a run for it.'

The three men ran to a chicken shed on the edge of the village. Just as they reached it, a missile released by a coalition warplane overhead slammed into it. Dust shot into the sky and the wooden boards of the shed tumbled through the air.

Serhad had kept up a constant rate of fire and was down to his last fifteen rounds. Two novice YPJ comrades next to me volunteered to resupply him. Serhad refused their help, saying there were jihadis all around him. 'I'll do it,' came a voice on the radio that I recognised as Jamal's. Before anyone could stop him, I saw Jamal darting through a grove of olives in front, taking a second comrade with him. The earth started exploding around him. I realised one of our Dushka gunners was blasting away at Jamal, thinking he was a jihadi.

'You're firing at Jamal!' I screamed into the radio.

Jamal came on the radio. 'That's not me, Azad!' he shouted. 'I'm shooting too!'

At that, everyone opened up on the two figures in the olive grove. I think even ISIS was firing at them. When I went to check on them later, I couldn't find a single part of their bodies which hadn't been hit. There were more holes than flesh.

We kept up the pressure for another hour or so. Finally the moment came for which we had waited. A large crowd of ji-hadis suddenly made a break to the west. As they ran into an open field, I did a quick count: thirty-seven. They were within easy range. I waited until they were close, then began firing. One. Two. Three. Four. Five. Six . . .

I had at least fifteen kills that day. Seven Islamists escaped, though most of them were quickly picked off from the air. The field through which they ran was carpeted with bodies. We had waited so long to capture Misko, and we made them pay a price for that.

*

The last few weeks before Tolin relieved me went by in a waking dream of exhaustion. New memories still come back to me every now and then, but mostly only fragments. After Zuli suffered a near miss in an RPG strike, I finally convinced him to go home to Hungary. I have a memory of it snowing a few days later. Then I was nearly hit in the face by a Dushka round: the splinters from the wall next to me shot into my cheek. I also recall coming across a mine in the road over which we had all walked a hundred times.

One night a house where a group of five of our fighters were based was blown to smithereens. In the usual manner, they had lit a fire to distract ISIS from where they planned to spend the night – but the site they had chosen for their blaze was on top of a mine connected to a series of other explosives that the enemy had rigged up all around the house. I spent an hour gathering up fingers, eyeballs and lumps of flesh and placing them on five separate blankets, trying to put them back together.

I also have a memory of following the roar and howl of an animal through a village at night. Eventually, the noise led me to an empty swimming pool behind a grand stone house. In it was a wild-looking dog, fat, dirty, growling and showing me his teeth. Next to him was a pile of human bones and two YPG uniforms. I lowered a bucket of water into the pool to give the animal something to drink. Then I found a plank and lowered it in so that it made a gangway for the dog to leave. Two days later when I returned, the dog was gone and we were able to collect the remains of our comrades.

The trauma would hit me much later, but at the time I functioned like an animal, just instinct and purpose. One day I noticed I had even developed the habit of pissing every time we took over a new position, as though I was marking my territory. It was also around then that we received new battle orders. We were to stop allowing ISIS to escape. What the instruction didn't say, but what we understood, was that we needed to end the war. We were to kill or capture them all.

One day I ran into Herdem and Yildiz at our new sniper base behind the front. Yildiz only managed a brief greeting: she was stopping by to pick up more ammunition. Herdem wanted me to meet some foreign volunteers who had recently arrived, an Algerian-Italian called Karim, a Spanish revolutionary from Madrid and an American called Keith Broomfield from Massachusetts. Keith told me he had once been to prison but was now making a conscious choice to side with right against wrong. He had found his cause in the Kurds' fight against ISIS, he said. I liked Keith, and he was a great shot. There was something about his enthusiasm that reminded me of who I once was.

Such interludes, however, were only brief distractions from what had now become an obsession: washing in the Euphrates. I stank, and was dressed in filthy rags. For weeks I had tried to have a shower, only to be interrupted by a new firefight just as I prepared to step under the bucket. I felt encased in dirt and gore. I had to break out. I had to get clean.

One night we were advancing on the last village before the Euphrates when I found myself almost feverish with thirst. As we checked one house, then another, I asked for spare water but there was none. My knees began shaking. I slowed to a crawl, managing only one or two hundred metres at a time before I had to rest. When the sun started to rise around 5 a.m., my comrades spotted two litre-bottles of water and passed them to me. I drank one, then the other, then grabbed a child's blanket and, barely able to walk, hauled myself up onto a roof with a clear view of the Euphrates on which two YPJ were keeping watch. I sat up against a wall, wrapped my arms around my rifle, and tugged the blanket around me. 'If they attack,' I said to the two women, 'just leave me here. I can't move.' One of the women began to object but at that point I fainted.

I awoke sweating, with the sun on my face. There was a mattress underneath me, a large blanket on top of me, a lit wooden stove in the corner and a large red apple placed carefully on the ground nearby. When I checked the time, it was 2 p.m. I rose, descended from the roof and walked out into an open field. I followed a path through some sugar-cane fields towards the river. After a while, I could hear the sound of the water. I could smell the damp earth and taste its coolness.

I turned a corner and there it was, wide and quiet and deep green-blue. I ripped off my jacket, then my scarf, then my boots and my socks and my T-shirt. I stood my Dragunov and my M16 against a bank of reeds. Spring was at its height and the sun was shining brightly. I walked leadenly towards the water, my feet sinking into the sand. The water was sharp and cold and clean. That freshness! That liberation! My people had found shelter in these curved riverbanks for millennia. The river's restless currents had been their source of life, its ever-flowing strength the renewal of their hope and the sustenance of their purpose. I cupped its waters in my palms and splashed my face. I drank and drank.

Finally, I opened my eyes. About five hundred metres downstream, two jihadis were sitting on a motorbike, watching me. I ran for my Dragunov. But before I could fire, they gunned the bike and disappeared into the sugar cane.

TWENTY-ONE

Kobani,

April–May 2015

Maybe I should have stopped at the Euphrates. Ever since Sardasht, immersing myself in cold river waters had felt to me like the promise of a new beginning. But the war wasn't done with me. I fought on for a few more weeks, dispatched to the eastern front to help hold the line against a deadly ISIS counter-attack against Hamza's old team, then sent back to the southwest to lead the operation to take the hills around Sarrin.

The way I was being called across ever larger distances reflected our success. We had stopped ISIS, turned them back and were on the point of throwing them out of Rojava. The momentum was with us. Within two more years, our forces and those of the Kurds in northern Iraq and the warplanes of the coalition would kill thousands more jihadis, destroy ISIS as a military force and reduce its territory to a handful of tiny, scattered holdouts. Our front had grown from a few houses and a few streets in Kobani to a line that was hundreds of kilometres long. I should have been enjoying our new freedom. Instead, I felt like something had to give and that it was going to be me.

215

After observing how my composure was deteriorating, General Tolin made my decision for me and sent me back to Kobani to await further instructions. I returned to the new sniper base, a farmhouse that sat alone on a hill to the southwest of the city. The first days of summer would soon be upon us, the sky was a clear blue, the hills had turned from brown to green and the wind was heavy with the fragrance of fresh jasmine. All around the farm were fields of yellow daisies and red poppies and dark-blue lupins, like the patterns on the dresses my mother made when I was a boy. From the window of the car that took me there, I watched a pair of sparrows noisily building a nest in a tree beside the road, fighting speckled wheatears and crows for pieces of straw and grass. Surrounded as we were by the meat and metal of battle, you could imagine that the war had defiled all existence. Yet here was Nature, oblivious and eternal.

The base was manned by the same fighters who had been with us through Kobani: an anxious young YPG apprentice who always wanted to head for the front, and an elder man who seemed completely broken. By chance, Herdem, Yildiz and Nasrin were at the farmhouse when I arrived. I greeted them, then excused myself. I was finally leaving the front, and I needed to digest the moment alone. I cleaned my Dragunov one last time, then climbed with it up onto the roof. I laid the weapon in my lap and ran my hands over it. How many men had it killed, even before me? Where had it been? What had it seen? I respected this machine. It had been a good companion and a lifesaver. I took my saviour bullets out of my pocket, cleaned them, and put them back. Then I descended and leant my rifle carefully against the wall. Tolin had radioed ahead and I was glad I didn't have to explain myself to the others.

Coming back from the front, I had prepared myself for bad news. It had been three months since we took Kobani and I was bound to have missed the deaths of comrades that I knew. But I also felt it was impossible to ask who was alive and who was not. Who knew where the question might lead? There was also something ugly about enquiring about tragedy. I couldn't find the words. Instead, I resolved to wait until my friends decided on their own to tell me what they knew.

I might have expected Yildiz to be the one to talk. She was always so chatty; Herdem and Nasrin were far quieter. But in the event Yildiz was too distracted. She had been given a note asking her to return to the mountains in North Kurdistan for more training and she was busy packing. So it fell to Herdem and Nasrin to tell me about Zahra.

Zahra had been killed with another YPJ fighter on 29 January, two days after we liberated Kobani. She had been opening the shutters on a shop in a village outside the city when an ISIS mine rigged as a booby-trap exploded and cut them both in two. I received the news in silence. Zahra was such a pure and clean spirit, always smiling or labouring on a new base or putting up a new curtain or taking over a new place. She hardly slept. It took years of struggle and will for Zahra to become who she was. It seemed impossible that she could be gone in a second.

But I knew it was true. In peacetime, news of a disaster is often telegraphed in advance and you have time to steel yourself. But in Rojava, normal rules did not apply. I had seen the colour of death and I knew it could happen to anyone. We had learned to brace ourselves around the clock for bad news. Friends with whom we had the most intense and truthful relationships could be shot or crushed or ripped to pieces a kilometre away from us, and we wouldn't know for months. That was the way of this war. We mourned our friends late and alone, brought to a sudden halt by a single word during a chance conversation, or by happening across a list of the dead, or by catching sight of a photograph on a wall of martyrs. You could set your mind to endure hardship, starvation, killing and even dying. To volunteer for that kind of sacrifice had a nobility to it. But to survive the war, I was discovering, was to be rewarded with a lifetime to ponder the ways in which it had soiled us. That was our penance for living.

Zahra, my brave and cheerful friend. I didn't forget you. I didn't mean to miss our last goodbye. The scars your death carved on my heart are like marks on a stone tablet. Zahra, they didn't tell me you were gone.

Herdem said he had other news. Gentle, resolute, undaunted Hayri had died about a month after Zahra. He had been helping to take over a village when a sniper's bullet found him.

Coming on top of my grief for Zahra, the news was almost too much to swallow. It didn't make sense. Hayri was so unlikely a candidate for death. He was so careful, so calm. He had committed to pull the trigger whenever it was required and there was nothing that would keep him from his task. But it often seemed to me like he had saved a part of himself from the war to keep clean and pure. I knew the war was uncaring and thoughtless and that it took without plan or justice or remorse. I had also known that Hayri would survive. It seemed impossible that he had miscalculated. And if he was gone, if the war had managed to hunt down and kill one of its masters, then even what little I thought I knew about it was untrue. I couldn't digest it. Under my feet, I felt the universe slew. I was sure that Hayri might walk around the corner any minute and, in his knowing way, tease me about my scarf.

Then Nasrin spoke up. 'Hayri was like my brother,' she said. 'We came to Kobani together from our positions in Shengal, joking that we were sister and brother. But on the way, through everything that happened here, it became true. By the end, he really was my brother. I really feel that.'

It was the first time I had heard Nasrin really speak. Her words explained the silence that she and Hayri shared. It was something that they had arrived at together. It seemed they had agreed early on to an unspoken pact of calm, reserve and empathy to get them through what lay ahead. It had made them family. It had sustained them through all those months lying alone behind their guns in the rubble. I felt I understood it. If neither of them articulated the horror out loud, if only innocence and light passed between them, then it would have felt like there was a chance that they would pass through this hell unbroken. There was even the chance that they might reclaim the lives they'd once had. But now Hayri was gone, and Nasrin was alone, and the promise they had made one another was dead.

Herdem and I watched Nasrin. She grew restless, as if she regretted talking. Oh, Hayri, I think she felt she had betrayed you by talking. Did you know how she loved you, Hayri? What spite in this war, to bring us together only to tear us apart.

Nasrin began packing her gear. That afternoon she left to go back to the front. I sat with Herdem as he checked his kit and handed out instructions. After a while, I asked, 'Who is going to replace me at the front?'

Herdem didn't reply. He just sat there. The losses were

weighing ever heavier on him and here was I presenting him with another one. My departure from the front would also mean no more radio talks between us. But Herdem didn't say a word. He never showed me the trouble my leaving might make for him nor tried to make me stay. He was wise and he understood exhaustion and the impact war could have on people. He knew from one look at me that I couldn't continue, and he accepted it.

Herdem let me stay at the snipers' headquarters for a few days. Eventually, Tolin came to say that she had a new assignment for me. Word about how we had stopped ISIS had travelled and the numbers of foreigners now showing up to volunteer or find out about the YPG and the YPJ meant the defence minister in Kobani needed someone to run an office of foreign affairs. 'You speak their language and know their culture,' said Tolin. I told her I would do what was needed.

As I gathered my things, I remember watching Yildiz finish her packing for the mountains. As ever, she was sunny, efficient and organised. There was no question that she would always serve the movement, wherever they needed her, whenever they asked. She left that night for the border and crossed over into North Kurdistan. Later, I would wish I had watched her go so I had the memory to hold on to. Dear Yildiz, my commander and protector, our sweet companion in the ruins, I don't remember if we said goodbye.

TWENTY-TWO

Kobani,

May–June 2015

After dialling the number for my parents' house, I listened to the ring. A woman's voice answered.

'Hello?'

I said nothing. I had not spoken to my family for two years. I wasn't sure I recognised the voice.

'Hello?' the voice asked again. It was my mother.

I didn't know where to begin.

'Is that you, Sora?' she asked. 'Sora?'

'Yes,' I said.

I could hear my mother breathing heavily. She started crying. It was a minute before she spoke again.

'How are you?' she asked. 'Are you OK? Are you wounded?'

'I was wounded a few times but not badly,' I said. 'I am alive. I am not bad.'

'I knew you were wounded!' she shouted. 'I had a dream.'

'Tell me about your dream,' I said.

'I was holding you as a baby in this room,' she said. 'There was a noise. I went out into the corridor and there were two demons there. They were walking past. I thought to myself: "I don't want my baby to see these distorted, wicked faces. And I don't want them to find my baby." So I stood there, blocking the doorway.

'The first demon looked at me right in the eyes and passed on. As the second one was passing, he looked over my shoulder into the room and saw my baby. I tried to stop him but he pushed past me. He went for you. I went for you. We were both holding you, the devil trying to take you away and me trying to save you. Then the other demon came and stabbed me in the back with a knife. I screamed and woke up, shaking and panicked. I knew something had happened to you.'

It was unnerving to hear my mother's dream, so fantastical and strange. But she was also a mother talking to her son about the nightmares he was giving her, and in a way the dream made some sense. Something about two devils in a corridor, the way the second one turned and attacked, reminded me of the two jihadis outside the cultural centre, the boy and the man, running down the street. 'Don't worry, mother,' I told her, 'I'm all right. I met your devils. One of them wounded me. I killed one and wounded the other. I got away. I'm doing fine. I am walking.'

To prove it, I took a picture of myself and sent it to her.

Herdem had a new truck that he had taken from a group of jihadis he had killed. He dropped me the next morning at the yellow-and-grey Syrian government building we had commandeered for our defence ministry.

The minister was Xhalo, an old man from Kobani, who was kind, respectful, meticulously organised and neatly dressed. My clothes were filthy from months of fighting and my trousers still had holes in their legs where I had been caught by small shards of shrapnel. But Xhalo pretended not to notice and even allowed me to take a mattress and a blanket up to the roof at night so that I could stay there, out in the open.

Aside from the few times when I had collapsed from exhaustion, I hadn't slept for more than a few minutes at a time for months. Now, when I tried to sleep indoors, I found it impossible. My mind had been in the war for too long. Walls blocked my view of the battlefield. Floors were unsafe. But roofs were good for seeing what might be coming. And so for months, like a bird, I returned each night to my nest on top of the ministry.

I had lost so much weight, my teeth were destroyed by lack of brushing and too much coffee, I had developed a near-permanent sniper's squint, and I couldn't eat more than a morsel. But that didn't account for the ache in my stomach. My belly seemed to be able to hear the suffering and pain of the war. When people spoke, I heard them with my ears but with my guts, too. The biggest injury was to my heart. It was howling, day and night. I tried to be kind to it. I told my mind to respect my heart, to listen to it, because I had locked it away for so long and now that I had released it, it needed to scream and shout.

In a strange way, I found myself missing the front. My comrades. The narrow focus. The lack of choice. Now that I was no longer there, I felt the absence of war, the lack of a force pushing me through its narrow channels of exigency. I had the freedom to do what I wanted – the freedom, after all, for which I had fought. But I was unused to it. I was like a pilot sitting on the runway with the chance to fly anywhere but finding he had lost all feel for the controls. I had been at peace in war, I realised. Now I was at war in peace.

As I hesitated, I felt the weight of my experience begin to crush me. This war was not something we had planned. It had been imposed on us. It was a reality far bigger than our own. And now that I was able to look back at it, I was starting to sense the size of it and how its immensity might overwhelm everything that I was. Nor had I left the fighting entirely behind. Part of me, I knew, wanted to hold on to it. I wanted to feel that kinship with my comrades. I wanted my injuries to last to keep me sharp. And in Kobani, of course, I was still in the middle of a battlefield of which I knew every brick and every hole. All my instincts told me that the dark and quiet were merely a lull in the fighting. At any moment, a word or a gesture or a sound could transport me back to the front and I would be stuck there for hours at a time. I tried to convince myself that it was over. Then I tried not to try. But my body knew better. I was still at war. It raged inside me.

When I could, I took walks around Kobani. Looking around the streets, viewing all the destruction, I felt the old fury. Why would anyone choose to destroy my land as their way to heaven? How could anyone imagine vandalism as a path to paradise? They had wrecked our city. They had killed over a thousand of us, wounded another two thousand and sent hundreds of thousands more fleeing as refugees. I was angry that even one of these imbeciles might have died with the illusion that my bullets were sending them to a glorious afterlife. I didn't want them to think I was giving them anything but the pain they inflicted on us.

If I wasn't sleeping, which was often, I would walk at night. I had discovered so many new things in this war, things which I would not have absorbed in two hundred years of living, and like a curious child I found myself returning to the places of my learning. The war had been a cruel explosion of understanding: what friendship means, what comrades are, what an enemy is, what it means to say 'our land' and 'our people' and 'life and death'. I went back to the cultural centre. I went to the girls' school. I went to the Black School. I went to Forty-Eighth Street and Mistenur Hill. I walked the rooftops and lay down in my old bases. I spoke to bricks, to houses, to streets, to broken doors and empty chairs. Sometimes I would see a person in the far distance and my finger would reach for a trigger and I would stay there for a while, remembering how I had lain in that place for three or four days, just watching and waiting for my shot.

But the city was mostly empty. My comrades were no longer there, nor ISIS, and I could walk freely in the streets. I developed the habit of lying down in the open and looking up at the night sky, trying to accustom myself to the calm and peace. And over the weeks and months of my wanderings, as I watched families start to return to their homes, I began to see that death had lost interest in Kobani and that maybe there was the possibility of something new. This was how it was when a place came back to life. This was how it felt to have the opportunity to live again. This is what it was to be reborn. One thing of which I was certain was that, from now on, I would live with deeper meaning. My understanding of life, people and family had changed. Fear, death, freedom and love would remain my closest confidants. And that knowledge, I was beginning to realise, could light my new path forward.

Many times I found myself returning to the city graveyard. The long lines of bodies buried next to each other seemed to insist on regular visits. I would read the names: who they were, how they had died, places and dates. There were so many I hadn't met. Young ones, old ones, men, women, children, all filling the earth. I would stay for hours, lying down between the graves, conversing with my comrades.

I had heard about survivor's guilt. I wasn't sure I had it, not exactly. Why I'd lived and why others had died – and what that said about me, that I could walk out of a war, that I was good at war – remained a mystery to me. My idea was that war was not really living. It was surviving by instinct, a sharpness that was more animal than human. Now that I was becoming human again, I could talk to my comrades as people too. I would tell them that I was still willing to die a hundred times for honour and respect, liberation and history, to live a life free from backwardness and blind ideology. But I was also preparing myself for a different existence. It wasn't easy. I could feel that the souls of my comrades were at peace. I knew I was not.

I was out among the graves one day when I received a call telling me that Herdem had been shot. He had been leading an advance on a village where ISIS were still holding out. At one point, a breach opened up in their defences and Herdem jumped into it. He survived, as ever. But hours later, after that battle was won, Herdem walked into a house that he imagined to be empty and was confronted by two terrified ISIS fighters. They had hidden away during the fighting. I imagine it wouldn't have occurred to Herdem that anyone could be so cowardly. He took a single bullet in his upper right arm which passed through his lungs and heart before exiting through his other side.

Herdem's body was taken to a makeshift hospital in the city. I radioed Nasrin, who was on the southern front, and she came back immediately so that we could go together to see him. When we arrived, we found our fellow sniper Haroon already there. He had been close to Herdem. As they moved his body into the back of the truck, Haroon taped Herdem's black Dragunov to the bonnet.

By now a number of comrades had arrived and we set off in a procession from the hospital to the graveyard. Some of us fired guns in the air. After twenty minutes we arrived and I helped carry Herdem's body to a spare patch of ground at the end of a line of graves. We dug a trench for him in the yellow soil, then lowered him in. Once he was inside the grave, I helped the grave-diggers stack breezeblocks over his body to make a stone coffin.

It was my job to cover Herdem's head. As I was placing some bricks over the last few gaps, watching his face disappear, our last conversation came back to me. 'How can I send you to the front and rest back at headquarters?' Herdem had asked. Herdem had always done what he said, right up until his death. He met that commitment with his life. And it was Herdem who taught us that a bullet doesn't know addresses or colours or ages, or care whether you are a poor man or a president. He had accepted the fate that he knew awaited him. But as I heard his voice one more time, I broke down, splitting open right inside his grave. I cried and cried. They had to pull me out.

I sat there with Nasrin next to the hole as they filled it with earth and then, one by one, started to drift away. Eventually, the two of us stood up and walked back together into the city which, more than anyone, Herdem had helped to liberate.

TWENTY-THREE

Kobani,

July 2015 to April 2016

By now, thousands of Kobani's townspeople were pouring back into the city. There were shortages of everything: food, milk, petrol, blankets, doors, windows. There were also still thousands of mines, booby-traps and unexploded mortars lying around the city. Every day, someone would be killed by the presents ISIS had left behind, many of them children. Within a few weeks of my returning, the total number of civilians who had died this way stood at thirty-three. We were also steadily losing our mine-clearers: from an original squad of twenty-three we were down to four or five.

Many of the new arrivals were looking for loved ones who had fought in the war. Mothers looking for daughters, wives looking for husbands, brothers asking after brothers. People would see the devastation around them and understand that to search through such chaos might be fruitless. That just made them more desperate. Day after day, more came. Every hour we were in the office, Xhalo and I would find ourselves wading through another family tragedy. Xhalo would just look out at his town and cry. I found that the blood and the horror of conflict had prepared me for my new work. I would listen, then try to find out information on the missing from our martyrs' committee, or from the front, or from friends and comrades I knew. If we had luck, I would take these people out to the graveyard and show them where their lost ones lay. Often I couldn't help. Sometimes volunteers had died even before they had picked up a rifle, before anyone knew their name. Sometimes there was nothing left of them, or no one left alive who might have known what had happened to them. And we had no archive that had made it whole through the war. I would lead these families of the vanished to the section of the graveyard where the headstones were just marked with numbers and dates. There were hundreds of them. It was all I could do.

One time I accompanied a YPG committee to Qamishli and the old neighbourhood where I used to be an administrator. We were there to tell the mother of a comrade that her son had died. All the way there we struggled with the weight of the news we had to deliver.

When we arrived, at first the mother misunderstood our reason for coming, dropping everything she was doing to welcome us inside her home, so happy and excited to be visited by so many friends and comrades of her son. We sat there in silence while she busied herself making tea. Some of us looked at the ground. Some stared at this strong, bustling woman whose life we were about to ruin. None of us knew how to start. Then she sensed something. Her face fell and became white. She started shaking. The glasses of tea rattled and spilled in her hands. Finally, one of the comrades broke the silence.

'Your son has been martyred,' he said.

I was the youngest-looking among the group. After a while, the woman gathered herself, looked me in the eyes, took my hands and said, 'I wish the years my son never had to you. You live your life for him.'

Kobani, July 2015 to April 2016

*

Arriving with the returnees were hundreds of foreigners: activists from Spain, politicians from Germany, film-makers from Chile, journalists from America, France, the UK and China. It felt like another kind of assault, and at the office of foreign affairs I was on the frontline of it. The journalists were writing articles and essays, interviewing people, filming the city, asking us how it was, how we felt, if we had lost anyone, what age we were, how our friends had died and how to spell our names. Sometimes I would watch the international news on CNN and the BBC. They all seemed to be talking about Kobani.

I tried to be as efficient and courteous as possible, finding out who these people were and what they wanted, offering them a glass of tea, telling them brief details of a battle or two, then trying to send them on their way. Many of them would realise that I had spent time at the front. 'You are the one we need,' they would say.

I always refused to be interviewed, as did many of my comrades. From the beginning, I found it hard to respect the journalists. They professed to be fascinated by our bravery. Actually they just wanted to steal our stories. I found it disrespectful that they would appropriate our lives in this way and sell us as if we were commodities. They called us 'victims' or 'rebels' or even 'packages'. Everything we had done was, for them, the way they made a living. They would listen eagerly and write down every word but it was all just a brief assignment before they moved on to other people and other wars. When I saw their excitement as they listened to us, it wasn't because of what we had done or what we stood for. They were just happy to have copy. They found bloodshed thrilling or heroic, or even beautiful. They said our women snipers were 'cool' and 'hot'.

231

One journalist proposed sticking a tiny camera on my rifle and filming as I shot jihadis. It was obscene. What we had been through was terrible and ugly. It was not a movie. To me, most of these people seemed little more than thieves.

It all made me extremely nervous around journalists. I told them I did not have the time to talk, which was true, or that I didn't want to talk, which was also accurate. For most of two years I had done nothing but look for the enemy and try to figure out how to attack and how to defend. I found it difficult to talk to anyone who had not been directly affected by the war. It was impossible for me to be interested in problems such as live feeds and deadlines.

I also believed that the right to tell your own story, to get it right, to tell the truth as only you knew it and only you could know it, was a fundamental human freedom. In the end, I came to like some of these foreigners, those who approached me with the genuine intent of learning and sharing, and some of them even became friends. But telling my story was how I defined myself in the world. None of these people knew where we had been. They didn't know how we had fought street by street, house by house. They barely knew who we were. No one was going to tell that story for us. For them even to imagine they could only showed how little they knew.

One day a journalist who was trying to interview me asked me if I realised that the whole world had been looking at Kobani as we fought. His words confused me. In battle, we had had no sense of anything beyond the street where we were fighting. The war had filled everything. We had fought out of simple necessity, because this was our land for which we would die. And because I was there, that was what I did. 'This is what we were assigned to do,' I responded blankly. 'We did what we had to.'

But the journalist's words stayed with me. Over the months I stayed in Kobani, I began to see what we had done as historic. In one way or another, more than a hundred countries had lent us their support in our fight against ISIS. The coalition had been almost unprecedented, bringing together nations such as the US and Russia who were enemies elsewhere, and even Turkey and Iran, who were killing their own Kurds at the time. I began to understand that the entire planet had realised ISIS was a threat. ISIS was backward and repressive and against civilisation – and, until we had stopped them, they had posed a threat to every corner of the world. When they attacked Mosul, a city of two million, five hundred of them took it in twenty-four hours. No one felt able to withstand their rage. You had to be suicidal to face suicidal. Only the YPG and YPJ proved up to the task.

There was something else. ISIS had been born from the American prisons in Iraq. And when you looked at who later joined their ranks, many coalition countries shared the blame. By some counts, ISIS had forty thousand volunteers from one hundred and ten countries around the world, including America, Canada, Germany, Australia, Britain and, especially, France. Often the jihadis were misfits in their home countries, disregarded and marginalised, petty criminals and dropouts. They had felt shunned in these other countries, but ISIS had given them a community and a brotherhood. It had drugged them with religion. It had even fed them actual narcotics: we found bags of ecstasy, heroin, cocaine and other drugs in the positions we captured from them. These countries had washed their hands of these feral, unwanted children. It had fallen to us to deal with their failure. No wonder the whole world appreciated what we had done. They owed us.

That didn't detract from the nobility of our fight. We had stood firm for enlightenment and principle, honesty and freedom. It had cost us dearly. But it had been the making of so many, too. I had seen this myself: how a weak character could become a strong commander. Our people had found themselves in this cause. And it was fascinating to me, how something born of catastrophe and from a small group of young Kurds committing themselves to a set of principles could be such an example to the world. Maybe, I thought, the war in Kobani had lit the beacon for Rojava.

Besides the journalists, there were thousands of other foreigners who came to see us: activists, actors, anarchists, artists, ecologists, economists, feminists, musicians, philosophers, political scientists, sociologists and writers. They saw us as revolutionaries of hope. They wanted to find out more about the ideas that inspired us. They wanted to stand next to us and against what was wrong.

That, too, was good. Ideas don't have a nationality. You don't have to be Russian to be a socialist, Greek to be a democrat or Tibetan to be a Buddhist. Ideas spread. People discover themselves in them. I had. When I first read Apo's books, I had been living in Britain long enough that I was not really Kurdish any more. I had come to recognise people, not race. I judged character. I valued ideas. When all these people arrived in Kobani, I felt I already knew why. Our philosophy is different from any other – how we view history, our ideas about democracy, feminism and anarchism, our attempt to be as close as is practically possible to real freedom. This is why others travelled so far to stand with us. Our principles had given me a sense of who I was, and they were doing the same for them. The appeal of Apo's ideas was not limited by border or race.

Many of the new arrivals became involved in our social, political, economic and media work, helping us to build our new society. Some of them fought with us, too. In the end, we received around four hundred military volunteers, from revolutionaries to former soldiers. Many had fought jihadis in Iraq or Afghanistan and Pakistan. They would say, 'Our governments should be doing more.' They had lost people, close friends, and they had come back to fight the same enemy again. Once we received a full team of five Americans: a BKC operator, an RPG man, a rifleman, a sniper and a medic. They had fought together in Iraq and now they had come to fight in Rojava. Another time, seventeen foreign volunteers arrived at once, including one man from Ukraine and another from China.

Of course, a few of them were adventurers, lost, loud people with big muscles looking for some new way for the world to see them. Some of them had been influenced by propaganda in their own countries: they told us proudly that they were there to kill Muslims. I would make these people wait a few weeks before I let them go to the front. Over that time I would see them change from wannabe killers to fellow comrades in a movement that wasn't so much against a group of jihadis as it was for a new way of living. I think the revelation, for them, was that we were not some mighty army of warriors but a group of volunteers standing up for our beliefs. Most of them also turned out to be decent people who had left their homes, friends and families, and comfortable, safe lives, to cross mountains, oceans and deserts to fight against injustice, cruelty and brutality. I gave them a phone and a laptop to share among themselves and insisted they call home every fortnight. When they wanted to leave, I gave them money for a ticket. Even if they hadn't achieved much, just by being there they were serving a purpose. Millions of Kurds had run away from their oppressors and their homeland. They were amazed to see foreigners fighting for them. It shamed them that they were trying to leave for Europe. It made many of them think again.

A number of these brave men and women died alongside us. One was Keith Broomfield, the American to whom Herdem had introduced me. In the few months he was with us, Keith built a reputation as a great sniper and a hard worker. He was shot by an ISIS sniper in early June 2015. My respect for his sacrifice is beyond words, not least because Keith never lived to see the change for which he fought. We named the foreign volunteers' headquarters in Kobani after him.

There was another, older volunteer called Gunter Helsten. Gunter was fifty-five and had served in the German army and the French Foreign Legion, for whom he had commanded troops in Africa and Asia. 'For all those years, I was fighting for governments and for business people – for money,' he said. 'Eventually I came to understand that as a soldier, my duty was to protect women and children. So I stopped.'

When he read about us, Gunter put his house in Luxembourg in his sixteen-year-old son's name and travelled to Kurdistan to help us. He said he wasn't there to fight against ISIS but to stand shoulder to shoulder with the Kurds. He was a disciplined and principled man who would wake up every morning at half past four to take a cold shower. He told me that when his son's class had been asked to write about their hero, his boy had written about him – who he was, what he was doing and how his son had taken a long time to understand why he was doing it – and had won a prize for his essay. You never saw a father so proud.

Because of Gunter's experience, Tolin asked him to set up a military training academy. Gunter agreed but eventually went to the front when the supplies he needed were delayed. In early 2016 he was killed while taking part in an operation to take the last village held by ISIS on the border between Syria and Iraq, a successful advance which split ISIS' forces into two tiny strongholds. When I heard the news, I felt like I had lost an older brother.

*

Through the end of 2015 and into 2016, Kobani was coming back to life. We had workers cleaning the city, clearing away the bodies and moving debris off the streets. A group of British de-miners from the Mines Advisory Group arrived. They collected an enormous pile of explosives and ordnance, dumped it all in an area they dug outside the city the size of a small football pitch, and detonated it.

The more normal life became, the more I found that I was troubled by it. Instinctively, I wanted Kobani to stay as it was, as a museum and a tribute to my fallen friends and comrades. I hadn't known the town before the war. I only knew it as a battleground, a place of dust and blood, and people in green and black. For thousands of us, this place had been our whole lives. For the dead, these ruins would be everything they would ever know. It was a shock to realise that the debris would all soon be cleared away and that any memory of what had happened here would begin to fade.

I wasn't the only one who felt like that. One afternoon I went to see the site of an old battle, a building where I had lain for days, and I found a young couple with a baby busy cleaning what remained. 'Are you here to see the house?' the man asked, unprompted. It seemed he had already been visited by several other comrades returning to the scene of the fight.

I looked inside their home. There were no windows, no doors, no locks, no fridge, no oven, and out in the garden the flowers and trees were dead. Everything they knew had been destroyed. The young man and his wife had tried to live in the camps but said they found it too hard. They had come back to their home and, although nothing was what it had been, they said they preferred it. 'In the camps, we never knew what was happening,' the woman said. 'We could hear the explosions. We couldn't sleep. At least now we can see what has happened.'

The couple, I realised, had come back to rebuild their memories. They couldn't bear to see what the place had become. And, of course, they were right to do so. We needed people to come home and reconstruct so that normal life could resume. But there was no escaping the fact that in order to restore their world they would have to destroy mine. In the end it was decided that the cultural centre and a few nearby blocks should be preserved as they were when I knew them. They stand there to this day, wrecks in the middle of the city, a piece of battlefield into which people can step and walk around and smell the dust into which so many of us bled.

One day I received the news that Yildiz had been killed in the mountains. Turkey considers any mountain Kurd they find actually living in those mountains to be a terrorist. A Turkish warplane was said to have spotted the truck in which she and a group of nine other YPJ fighters were travelling to a training camp and attacked it. None of them, we were told, survived.

Of our original group of five snipers, only Nasrin and I remained alive. Nasrin was still at the front. In my grief at Yildiz's loss, I suggested to Tolin that I return to fight alongside her.

'You're looking for an easy job?' she replied.

I must have looked stunned.

'You'd be running away from this important new duty,' said Tolin. 'This is your new battleground, dealing with these people, helping them, fixing things. Is it that you think this war cannot go on without you? Do you think you are the only one who can save us?'

Tolin, I recognise now, was trying to save me from the habit of war. At first, the fighting had been terrifying. When I first shot someone and saw them die, I had nightmares for weeks. But the second time I killed someone, I had maybe one or two dreams; the third time I had one; by the fifth, there were none. Like anything, you adapt to killing. It can even become an addiction. Tolin could see the front was calling to me. She knew that if I answered the call, I might finally lose my humanity. 'If you just fight at the front without understanding, it doesn't matter what you achieve there,' she told me. 'You will end up as nothing more than a killer, a criminal. Yes, you will be fighting ISIS. But you will be just as trapped as they are.'

Our movement was only too aware of the dangers of comrades becoming addicted to fighting and had a programme to deal with it. Even the most senior commanders would be sent back from the front and asked to take charge of a small village. The idea was to remember normal life and everyday things. I began to practise my own version of this process, visiting the villages outside Kobani. The people would talk about goats and vegetables. I expected it to be dull. But when I was there, I found it so pleasurable. All these emotions wrapped up in something so small – there was something simple, beautiful and profound about it. I discovered I could keep my fierce principles – beliefs I was ready to die for – without having to ignore life. These people were who I had been as a boy growing up with my family in Sardasht. I loved to hear the mothers talking about how they made yoghurt and tomato puree. They were perfectionists, and there was wisdom, calculation and planning in everything they did.

Later, when I returned to Europe and to Leeds, I would remember these villages. Watching my friends becoming excited about what clothes they wore and what TV channel or film to watch and slapping each other on the back as they enjoyed a meal, I would tell myself that their happiness was beautiful, and the common ground on which all people can come together. This was life. War was something else. The only good reason to fight, really, was to allow people in Kurdish villages or northern British cities or anywhere else to live as they wanted, as they always had, as they chose to.

I spent a year in Kobani. At the end of my time there, I began to think of writing my story. When I talked to journalists, they would encourage me. I also remembered the words of the husband of my teacher in Leeds and how he said I could become a writer one day.

When it came to why we fought, our thoughts had always been as clear as a mountain stream. For me, it was the result of a simple quest for freedom that started when I was a boy. I had wanted what any human being wants: to live with honour and dignity. The search led me to some dark places. I had to confront the most malevolent and misguided men. I had to watch so many friends die. But maybe telling the story of Kobani was a way to make the sacrifice serve a wider purpose. For decades, Turkish and Iranian propaganda had made it so hard for us to be heard. But Kobani earned us worldwide respect. In forty years we had not achieved the kind of recognition that we did from those five months. The reason Kobani connected with people was, I think, because such a pure story of free will offered them powerful and universal inspiration. Because being right didn't always mean winning. The good and progressive does not inevitably triumph over the bad and backward. We had to make sure it did. And perhaps there is no more meaningful and moving story than a never-say-die struggle for human freedom.

TWENTY-FOUR

Silemani, Frankfurt, Brussels and Leeds,
2016–2018

I left Kobani one morning in April 2016. I took off my green trousers and jacket and pulled on some jeans and a T-shirt. It made my head spin. I was removing the uniform that had given us such pride and honour and stepping into the uniform of civilians the world over.

It was in something of a daze that I retraced the journey I had made two and a half years before, crossing back into Iraq, following the Tigris past Mosul and Kirkuk, until eventually I arrived at Silemani. My plan was to spend some time in the city to recover. I still hadn't gained much weight, my teeth were bad and I wasn't sleeping more than an hour a night. After a few months in Silemani, I planned to travel on to Europe.

In Silemani, I began to wonder whether I could ever settle back into life in Britain. South Kurdistan already felt like another planet. Kurdish friends tried to give me bodyguards and a pistol – ISIS assassins might have been operating in the area – but I refused. I had an idea about passing my days in coffee shops or sitting on a park bench, smelling the kebabs at the roadside stalls and listening to the voices from the fruit market and the sound of birds in the trees.

But I overestimated my ability to blend in. I looked too old and too serious for my thirty-two years. When I walked down a street, I had a very stiff and deliberate way of stepping and I was always scanning for sniper holes and nests and vantage points. In a city of yellow stone houses and cafés on leafy squares, surrounded by towering green mountains, I found myself instinctively drawn to the best places from which to defend it.

My interactions with people were also a disaster. Walking into the city market, I would become overwhelmed by all the information I was picking up with my eyes and ears. When I tried to talk to people, I found I had no answer when they asked me how I was. When I lied and said I was looking for work, I could see them wondering what kind of work I did, exactly. I saw the same look when I walked into a restaurant or came to pay the bill. It was fear. I resolved to say as little as possible. I watched the way they drank grape juice from a glass and how they played with their coffee spoons and tried to copy them. I tried to talk the way they talked. But the way I stared at them just worried people even more, and when I shook their hand, it was like they could feel my true nature through my skin. I wondered if I would always be like this: the man who carried so much death with him that people shivered when he passed by.

In December, I flew to Frankfurt, Germany. Rojava's representatives in Europe had organised for a family to pick me up from the airport. They took me home, then the next day to one of the floating cafés on the river in the city. That was when the mother, Hekmat, told me her son had died in the war. She said she had two more sons in the YPG. She showed me a picture. It was Tolhildan.

Hekmat was the mother who had tried to save her son from the war and whom Tolhildan had forsworn, vowing the only way he would leave Kobani was in a box. In fact, Tolhildan had survived the city only to be shot dead weeks later in the villages. He had always been one of the fighters I most admired and his death had floored me. Now that I was in his mother's presence, the memories came flooding back so strongly – his face, his voice – that I had to leave.

I walked up the riverbank and sat on the grass next to the water. Everybody was going about their ordinary day. I sat in the middle of them, my mind filled with bodies and gunfire and battle. I was back in Kobani. Everything was returning to me so thickly that I didn't notice Hekmat's approach. She sat next to me and hugged me.

After a while, I told her a few things about her son. About when the Hummer came and how her son had stopped it. How disciplined he was. How old he looked.

Hekmat looked up at me and smiled. 'I am happy because I can still smell him on you,' she said.

Tolhildan's mother dropped me at the station and I took the train to Brussels, where there was another family to meet me. I felt even less at home in this city. It was a freezing-cold, grey European winter. I couldn't bear to be outside for more than a few minutes. I also found I couldn't taste the food. The cucumbers and tomatoes, all grown in greenhouses and packaged in plastic, had no substance to them. I began to lose my appetite again.

243

But finally, with the help of a few European friends I had met in Kobani, I began writing. That work continued when I moved back to Leeds in the autumn of 2017 and for the next year after that. It wasn't easy. Just as it would take time to stitch so many pieces of myself back together, so I realised it would take a couple of years to write down all my thoughts in a way that made sense.

It wasn't that my thoughts were disordered. My story, and the story of so many of us, was a straight line that ran directly from the moment when we first stood up against injustice. In my case, my journey had taken me from my childhood across the Middle East and Europe only for me to reverse course and travel back to my land to fight with my people in Kobani. And now I had seen free Kurdistan. No longer was our freedom a place in our imagination or on a few ancient maps. Now I knew it as a land across which I had walked.

The story of my people was just as linear. After resisting injustice and oppression for centuries, we had wrested our freedom from the hands of others. Kobani unified the Kurds from Turkey, Syria, Iraq and Iran. It also briefly unified the world behind us. And there was no reversing that moment. Finally, the Kurds were establishing themselves as a people. After Kobani, the idea of Kurdish freedom was alive again. Our destiny was once more our own.

I regretted more than anyone that it took calamity to bring us all together. But that we had triumphed over such suffering, that so few had stood with forty-year-old guns against so many with so much money and the best military equipment, and won – that made anything possible. While the battle for Kobani raged, in Turkey tens of thousands of Kurds began an uprising that continues to this day. In East Kurdistan, there were protests and uprisings, including days of clashes in Sardasht. In Iraq,

Kurdish authorities briefly created a stable society in the north. There were setbacks, of course, such as in late 2017 when the Kurds in northern Iraq lost much of their territory again in an Iraqi–Iranian advance, and in early 2018 when Turkey linked up with the jihadis in Afrin in southwest Kurdistan and bombed our forces from the air as the Islamists advanced on the ground. But for the first time, these counter-attacks felt desperate and, ultimately, in vain. In Rojava, the Kurds had established their sovereignty for the first time in thousands of years. Even if the place was one day overrun and swallowed up, there was no erasing it from people's minds. It couldn't be undone. It would endure for ever. I, and thousands of others, would make sure of it.

Crucially, this was no mere triumph of one nation or race over another, as so often happened in the Middle East. This was the emergence of a new stable and peaceful social order, a stateless, autonomous democracy blind to race, religion or gender, based on self-determination, a communal economy and harmony with the environment. Rojava was unique. It was democracy with a vengeance, and it quickly became an example to the Middle East and beyond.

This new world was symbolised, above all, by the idea of a free woman. Women were the vanguard of the revolution and the mothers guiding the birth of our new world. They had fought ISIS. They would defend Rojava against its enemies in Turkey, Syria, Iraq and Iran in the struggles to come. And if women were our warriors, Kobani was our proof that liberation was vital and enduring. Our people had tasted freedom, nothing could take that away, and word of our achievement was echoing out around the world. Over there, they do not live like us. Our dictators' days are numbered. In that place they call Rojava, the people are finally free.

*

I speak to my family from time to time these days. They seem well. My father always gave me his opinion and I know he would never have let me leave if he'd known where I would go and what I would become. But he also always let me have my independence and I think he has made his peace with my life as a revolutionary.

He and my mother know I will continue to fight for our cause. Since they are watched and their phones are listened to, neither of them can tell me what they think of my choices. But I do know that when they were visited by the Iranian authorities one day, my mother shouted gleefully at them, 'He is not a child, he is a free man. Catch him if you can!'

I know my parents would like me to start a family. It is not an ambition I can allow myself. One of the reasons we fought and died was to build a new world in which patriarchy, marriage and tradition are replaced by a commitment between soul-mates to share their lives. But unless you possess that one place where you can love and sleep and wake safely in the morning, unless you have a home, everything else must wait. Most of us are still foreigners where we live. We don't have that safe place where we can exist freely and raise our children with honour and integrity. I hope that won't always be the case. But for now, like forty-five million other Kurds, I am still waiting for a home.

From time to time I receive news from Kurdistan. Tolin still commands our forces in Rojava. Serhad fights on. We used to joke that to walk unwounded out of Kobani would be shame-ful, but Haqi has taken that to new heights with his fourth set of injuries. He, too, remains a commander on the frontline. Janiwar, who had never thought to pick up a gun before war came to Kobani, lives still in his home town with his wife and son. Nasrin has stepped back from the fighting for now to study politics and ideology in the YPJ academy. One day, after years of living with Yildiz's death, I was stunned to be told by some old friends that she had survived the air attack in which I heard she had died. She was badly injured, but after a few weeks of recuperation she, too, had resumed her duties.

I have taken up ice-skating again, something I first learned on the frozen ponds around Sardasht. I have also started visiting my old friend Shina, who, after years living underground in Iran, was eventually granted asylum in Britain and moved to Scotland. We go walking and camping and fishing in the mountains around Ben Nevis. It reminds us of the old days in Kurdistan. Somehow those paths feel more familiar than the streets of Leeds whose layout, to my surprise, I am having to learn a second time. It is almost as though my brain has jettisoned anything from the years when I drifted away from the movement. I find myself wondering how I could have really lived like that. A car, a flat, a shopping centre, a supermarket. It does not seem like me at all.

I always walked for the feeling of liberation it gave me, but these days I find it also stills my mind. It will take a lifetime to come to terms with the cost of Kobani. How that city was ruined. How many of us died. How many we killed. The lives I took myself. I have never strayed from the conviction that it was worth it, but that doesn't stop me from measuring the price.

Lately, I've found my mind goes back to a day, soon after Tolin sent me back from the front, when I was walking around the ruins, retracing my steps as I remembered the battles we'd fought. On that day, I went to the house where I had destroyed that beautiful Italian marble kitchen to make a platform to lie on. When I arrived, there was an old man there. He looked at me.

'You know my house?' he asked me.

'Yes,' I said. 'I fought here. For two weeks. I built this huge platform on your top floor.'

Now that I saw the man, I remembered the extent to which I had destroyed his home to build my nest. I had ripped down an antenna from the roof. I made holes in the walls. I stuck pipes in the floor. I ripped a door off its hinges. I brought blankets and mattresses out of the bedroom and put those on top of the door and tied the whole platform together with scarves. I used everything. I wrecked it all.

The old man took me upstairs, to the fourth floor, where I saw that everything was the same as I had left it.

'I keep it as a memory of what happened in my house,' he said.

'I built it,' I told him.

'Why did you need it?' he asked. 'What are the holes in the walls for?'

I explained to the old man about corridors and line of sight and my system of holes. 'I shot somebody here,' I said, pointing through one opening in the wall. 'And I shot somebody over there.'

The old man nodded. We descended the stairs to the kitchen. There were the broken marble counters and the sink that I had destroyed. The old man's wife was there. I could tell the kitchen had been important to her.

'You know, it was me who broke your beautiful kitchen,' I said.

'You must stay and have a coffee in this kitchen,' she replied.

Immediately I was consumed by guilt at the knowledge that I had taken her best coffee cups upstairs to use for drinking and dampening my shooting holes.

The old woman saw the look on my face. 'You didn't break everything,' she reassured me.

She found three cups, we drank our coffee, and I tried to tell her and her husband something about the war. But it was hard, and the old lady could see that I was embarrassed about what I had done to her home.

After a while she leaned over to me and patted me on the knee.

'You didn't break my house,' she said. 'You saved it.'

ACKNOWLEDGEMENTS

This book is the product of several years of writing, rewriting, reporting and re-reporting, and that it exists at all is due to the shared efforts of a wide cast of volunteers. First among them is Heval Tolin and Heval Haqi, my commanders in Rojava, and my friends. They not only saved me from myself innumerable times on the battlefield but also understood why I wanted to tell this story and excused me from duty for three months so that I could return to the scenes of the fighting and talk to others who were there with me. Today, Tolin and Haqi remain on the frontline fighting for Rojava and Kurdistan. It is their commitment and the determination of thousands like them that will ensure that one day we will have our freedom.

Also in Rojava, I need to thank my comrades Kazm, Roni, Baran and Koma for their assistance, and Santiago, Fouad Yassin and Salaam Amin, who first encouraged me to start writing. As a first-time writer, I leant on the expertise and support of many. Francesca Couchi helped me write my first chapter in Silemani and was always there to listen and offer insightful advice. Alba Sottorra Clua from Catalonia, who listened to my stories, coached me in structure and offered a critical review of the text. Jan Fermon in Belgium provided crucial legal advice. Anina Jendreyko in Switzerland and Narinder Khroud were generous with their views. Very special thanks is due to Renée In der Maur from the Netherlands, who I first met in Kobani in the first months after the war and who has always been there to help, teaching me basic computer literacy, setting aside weeks to help me with a proposal and reviewing all my drafts. For their generous welcomes, food, sympathetic ears, and spare rooms and sofas, I owe a great debt to Chia, Kamaran and Jyan, Himn and Azadeh, Rebwar, Nawzad and Farzaneh, and Delil in Brussels.

In New York, Servan Emiriki and Sue Hodson offered early support and corrective advice on my first poor attempt at a proposal. Virginia Marx offered early, insightful advice and made the connection to Patrick Walsh at Pew Literary, who became my agent. To Patrick and John Ash, I owe an unfathomable debt for seeing the potential in this book, championing it to the literary world and speedily assembling the large cast who have seen it through to publication around the world with integrity and great skill. In particular, Alex Perry, to whom Patrick introduced me, invested himself deeply and intensely in the formidable task of writing this book, putting himself entirely aside to melt into my story and find the voice and language to tell it. I am proud to say we now call each other 'brother', and he has my deepest respect and thanks.

I should also thank Morgan Entrekin, Brenna McDuffie and Alison Malecha at Grove Atlantic in New York for engaged and pinpoint editing. Paul Murphy at Orion in London offered generous encouragement and eagle-eyed reviews of the text, and Daniel Balado's copy-edit was extraordinary: precise, and brilliantly improving. I took great heart, too, from the early support of Margit Ketterle and Iris Forster at Droemer Knaur in Munich, Cristina Foschini at Mauri Spagnol and Giuseppe Strazzeri at Longanesi in Milan, Tom Harmsen at Uitgever in Amsterdam and my publishers at Kobunsha in Japan.

There are many more who are due my deepest and sincerest thanks but who, because of the way they might be treated by our enemies, must remain anonymous. My gratitude is only delayed, until we meet again and I can express it in person.